Everyday Life in
Homeric Greece

Everyday Life in Homeric Greece

Written and Illustrated by
Marjorie and C. H. B. Quennell

G. P. Putnam's Sons

New York and London

The Knickerbocker Press

1930

EVERYDAY LIFE IN
HOMERIC GREECE

Copyright, 1930
by
Marjorie Quennell
and
C. H. B. Quennell

Published, Spring, 1930

Made in the United States of America

TO

N. Q.

"*Let our artists rather be those who are gifted to discern the true nature of the beautiful and graceful; then will our youth dwell in a land of health, amid fair sights and sounds, and receive the good in everything; and beauty, the effluence of fair works, shall flow into the eye and ear, like a health-giving breeze from a purer region, and insensibly draw the soul from earliest years into likeness and sympathy with the beauty of reason.*"

THE REPUBLIC OF PLATO, BOOK III
(Jowett's Translation).

PREFACE

THIS book is intended for boys and girls of public school age. As it has been made on rather different lines from the others we have written, a short explanation of its aims may be necessary. To-day there is hardly a Science, or Art, whose beginnings cannot be traced back to Greece. In Architecture she still reigns supreme. Gothic is no longer a living style, and our cities are planned on a Renaissance, or rebirth, of classical design inherited from Greece through Rome. The most modern type of building, an American skyscraper, soaring into the air, to twice the height of St. Paul's in London, decorates itself perhaps with Ionic caps from the Erectheum in Athens.

In Sculpture the figures from the pediment of the Parthenon in the British Museum, and the serene archaic "Aunts" in the Acropolis Museum at Athens, are not disturbed by the crudities of the modern sculptor.

Homer laid the foundations of Literature in Western Europe, and Plato has guided all the philosophers who have followed him. Herodotus

Preface

and Thucydides founded schools of History. Wherever we turn we find that Greece led the way.

Hippocrates, born about 460 B.C., was not only a great doctor, but his oath defined for the first time the obligation of a professional man, to regard his work as more important than its monetary reward.

The engineers and technicians of to-day do all their calculations on principles discovered by the mathematicians of Greece. They substituted the "Rule of Knowledge" for "Rule of Thumb."

If this is the case, then it is obvious, unless we are satisfied with a narrowly vocational education, that we should know something of the History of Greece; but how is this to be done?

Hitherto, the approach to Greece has been solely by a literary channel, and few have been able to navigate it safely. Grammar and syntax have acted as Scylla and Charybdis. The Arthurs, of "Tom Brown's Schooldays," are outnumbered by the Slogger Williams, who, having no joy in words, regard their task as so much weary boredom; yet the Sloggers are often very useful people who might be caught in another way. This book is an attempt in that direction.

It seems to us that we all need a classical education, and it would be excellent if it could start in the elementary schools. Beginning with good translations, our boys and girls could be familiar-

Preface

ised with the beginnings of the Sciences and Arts, and interested in creative work. Who knows—we might raise up the spirits of great men. The old Greeks and Romans, the men of the fifteenth and sixteenth centuries, might come to our aid, and lead the way to another Renaissance of the creative spirit.

The Tom Browns and the Slogger Williams would be humanised, and the Arthurs could be left quite safely to pass on to their own literary haven.

If, as we think, the Greeks have educated the Old and New Worlds, then we must start with Homer, because he was the Educator of Greece.

In this book we have not attempted to do more than set the scene, and secure the atmosphere of his time. In the second book we shall deal with Archaic and Classical Greece.

We are indebted to our son Peter for the translations of "Argonautica," the "Iliad," and the "Odyssey."

MARJORIE and C. H. B. QUENNELL.

BERKHAMSTEAD, HERTS,
    August 1929.

RECOMMENDED BOOKS

TITLE OF BOOK	AUTHOR	PUBLISHER
Mycenæ	Henry Schliemann	John Murray, 1878
Tiryns	Henry Schliemann	John Murray, 1886
The Iliad of Homer	Lang, Leaf, & Myers	Macmillan & Co., 1919
The Odyssey of Homer	Butcher & Lang	Macmillan & Co., 1924
A Smaller Classical Dictionary	E. H. Blakeney	J. M. Dent & Sons, 1927
Atlas of Ancient and Classical Geography		J. M. Dent & Sons, 1925
Companion to Greek Studies	Leonard Whibley	Camb. Univ. Press, 1916
Apollonius Rhodius, The Argonautica	R. C. Seaton	Heinemann, 1912
The Shaft Graves and Beehive Tombs of Mycenæ	Sir Arthur Evans	Macmillan & Co., 1929
The Architecture of Ancient Greece	Anderson, Spiers & Dinsmoor	Batsford, 1927
Handbook of Greek and Roman Architecture	D. S. Robertson	Camb. Univ. Press, 1929
Greek and Roman Life		British Museum, 1920
Greek and Roman Antiquities		British Museum, 1920

xi

Recommended Books

TITLE OF BOOK	AUTHOR	PUBLISHER
The Trojan Women	Trans. by Gilbert Murray	Allen & Unwin, 1925
Les Illustrations Antiques de l'Iliade	Kazimierz Bulas	Lwow, Paris, 1929
The Archer's Bow in the Homeric Poems	Henry Balfour	Journal of Royal Anthropological Institute, Vol. LI., 1921
Projectile Throwing Engines of the Ancients	Ralph Payne-Gallwey	Longmans, Green & Co., 1907

CONTENTS

Contents

ILLUSTRATIONS

Illustrations

Illustrations

Illustrations

EVERYDAY LIFE

IN

HOMERIC GREECE

1

EVERYDAY LIFE
IN HOMERIC GREECE

CHAPTER I

THE ARGONAUTS

In any book which deals with Greece, the first name to be mentioned should be that of Homer. He was the great educator of Ancient Greece. Xenophon makes one of his characters in the "Symposium" say, "My father, anxious that I should become a good man, made me learn all the poems of Homer."

Herodotus, the father of History, who wrote in the fifth century B.C., opens his book with references to the voyage of the Argonauts and the Siege of Troy, and by the far more critical Thucydides, who wrote at the end of the same century, Homer was evidently regarded as a historian to be quoted as an authority. If we follow their example, we shall be in excellent company.

We will begin with the voyage of the Argonauts,

3

because in this tale we find the spirit of adventure and love of the sea, or rather use of the sea, which was to be so characteristic of the Greeks of classical times. We may be able to capture some of the atmosphere of that heroic age, when gods like men, and men like gods, lived, loved, and fought together.

As to our authorities on the adventures of the Argonauts, Homer does not say very much, evidently thinking that his readers would know all about them. This is shown in the twelfth book of the "Odyssey." "One ship only of all that fare by sea hath passed that way, even 'Argo,' that is in all men's minds, on her voyage from Æetes." Fortunately for us, the details which were in all men's minds were gathered together by Apollonius Rhodius, who lived in Alexandria in the third century B.C. The details we give are quoted from his book "Argonautica."

This opens with a scene at the Court of Pelias, King of Iolcus, in Thessaly, who is disturbed because he has heard from an oracle "that a dreadful doom awaited him—that he should be slain at the bidding of the man whom he saw coming forth from the people with but one sandal." When Jason arrives with only one sandal, having lost the other in the mud, it is not to be wondered at, that he found his welcome a little chilly. "Quickly the king spied him and, brooding on it, plotted for him the toil of a troublous voyage, that on the sea or among strangers he might miss his home-coming."

The troublous voyage was to sail to Colchis and find the oak-grove wherein was suspended the Golden Fleece, guarded by a dragon, and having found the Fleece, to bring it back. Here was a task worthy of heroes. Jason gathered together a band. First came Orpheus, the music of whose lyre "bewitched the stubborn rocks on the mountain-side and the rivers in their courses." Then Polyphemus who, in his youth, fought with the Lapithæ against the Centaurs, and Heracles himself came from the market-place of Mycenæ, and many others, sons and grandsons of the immortals.

The goddess Athene "planned the swift ship, and Argus, son of Arestor, fashioned it at her bidding. And thus it proved itself excellent above all other ships that have ventured on to the sea with their oars"—which only means that there was a streak of genius in the design of the "Argo," because genius is a gift from the gods.

Jason was appointed leader, and preparations were made for launching the "Argo." "First of all, at the command of Argus, they girded the ship strongly outside with a well-twisted rope, pulling it taut on both sides, that the bolts might hold the planks fast and the planks withstand the battering of the surge." The heroes then dug a trench down to the sea and placed rollers under the keel. Then they reversed the oars, putting the handles out-board, and bound them to the thole-pins, and the heroes, standing on each side of the boat, used the projecting handles of the oars to push the "Argo" down into the sea. Then the mast and sails were fitted, and they drew lots for the benches for row-ing, two to each bench.

"Next, heaping shingle near the sea, there on the shore they built an altar to Apollo . . . and quickly spread about it logs of dried olive wood." Two steers were brought and lustral water, and barley meal, and Jason prayed to Apollo to guide their ship on its voyage and bring them all back safe and sound to Hellas, "and with his prayer cast the barley meal." Heracles and Ancæus killed the steers. "Heracles struck one of the steers with his club in the middle of the brow, and dropping in a heap where it stood, it tumbled to the ground; Ancæus smote on the broad neck of the other with his brazen axe and cut through the mighty sinews; and it fell prone on both its horns. Quickly their comrades slit the victims' throats and flayed the hides; they severed the joints and cut up the flesh, then hacked out the sacred thigh bones, and when they had wrapped them about with fat, burnt them upon cloven wood. And Jason poured out pure libations."

This was the general practice. Sacrifices were offered to the gods on all important occasions.

6

The Argonauts

The sacred thigh bones were burnt in their honour, and the joints eaten by the people in the festival which followed.

Achilles, the son of Peleus, who was to become a great hero himself, was brought by his mother to see the departure.

After the heroes had feasted and slept, they went on board the "Argo" and sailed away "Eastward Ho," or, rather, rowed away. To the sound of Orpheus's lyre they "smote the swelling brine with their oars, and the surge broke over the oar-blades; and on this side and on that the dark water seethed with spume, foaming terribly under the strokes of the mighty heroes. The ship sped on, their arms glittering like flame in the sunlight, and, like a path seen over a green plain, ever behind them shone their wake.

"Presently they raised the tall mast in the mast-box, and fastened it with the forestays, pulling them taut on both sides, and when they had hauled it to the topmast, they lowered the sail." We cannot follow the Argonauts through all their travels, but the first part of their voyage was to Colchis, which, in Greek mythology, was situated at the eastern end of the Black Sea. There the Argonauts voyaged, hugging the shores as they went. They did not reach Colchis without adventure—heroes never do. In the Sea of Marmora they encountered insolent and fierce men, "born of

7

the Earth, a marvel to see for those that dwelt about them, each with six mighty hands that he raises, two springing from his sturdy shoulders, and four beneath, fitting closely to his terrible sides." The Argonauts were attacked by these Earth-children, but Heracles "swiftly bent his back-springing bow against the monsters, and one after another brought them to ground."

Then for twelve days and nights fierce tempests arose and kept them from sailing, so they sacrificed to Rhea, the mother of all the gods, that the stormy blasts might cease. "At the same time, at Orpheus's bidding, the youths danced a measure, fully armed, clashing with their swords on their bucklers."

At another time "around the burning sacrifice they set up a broad dancing-ring, singing, 'All hail, fair god of healing, all hail.' "

It was in the Cianian land that Heracles and Polyphemus were lost, while searching for Hylas, who had been carried off by a water-nymph, and so the heroes sailed without them. Here it was that the heroes made fire by twirling sticks.

They next arrived at the land of the Bebrycians, where they found that all strangers had to box with the King Amycus. Polydeuces stood forth as the Argonauts' champion. A place of battle having been selected, "Lycoreus, the henchman of Amy-cus, laid at their feet on each side two pairs of

B.M.

Fig. 2.—Heracles strangling the
Nemean Lion.

B.M.

Fig. 3.—Sacrifice.

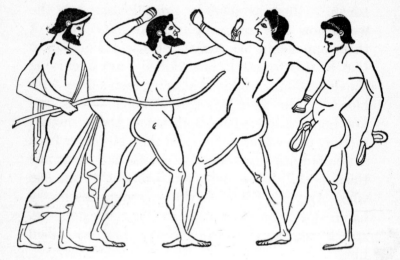

FIG. 4.—Boxers.

FIG. 5.—Prometheus.

gloves made of raw hides, dry and exceeding tough." Just as modern prize-fighters tell the world how they are going to make mince-meat of their opponents, so Amycus warned Polydeuces that he was to learn "how skilled I am in carving the dry oxhides, and in spattering men's faces with blood." The fight was truly heroic, "cheek and jaw bones clattered on both sides, and a mighty rattling of teeth arose, nor did they give over from fisticuffs until a gasping for breath had overcome them both." The fight was brought to an end when Amycus, rising on tiptoe, swung his heavy hand down on Polydeuces, who, sidestepping, struck the king above the ear and so killed him.

Their next adventure was in the Bithynian land, where they came to the assistance of Phineus, who was plagued by the Harpies, who came swooping through the clouds and snatched his food away with their crooked beaks. In return for their help, Phineus tells them of the dangers which still await them on the way to Colchis. So they were able to pass safely through the rocks which crashed together face to face.

It was in the land of the Mariandyni that Idmon, one of the heroes, was killed by a boar, and a barrow raised to his memory. Then they came to the land of the Amazons, but did not stop to fight the war-loving maids.

Next they came to the land of the Chalybes, who "take no thought for ploughing with oxen nor for planting any honey-sweet fruit; they do not pasture flocks in the dewy meadows. But they burrow the tough iron-bearing soil, and what they earn they barter for their daily food; never a day dawns for them but it finds them hard at work, amid drear sooty flames and smoke they endure heavy labour."

When they came to the island of Ares and its dangerous birds, "on their heads they set helmets of bronze, gleaming terribly, with tossing blood-red crests" as well; they had to hold their shields roof-wise over the "Argo" to defend themselves from the feathers which the birds there could discharge from their wings like arrows.

On and on they went, until "the precipices of the Caucasian Mountains towered overhead, where, bound on hard rocks by galling fetters of bronze, Prometheus fed with his liver an eagle that ever swooped back upon its prey. High above the ship in the evening they saw it flying close under the clouds, with a loud whir of wings. It set all the sails quivering with the beat of those huge pinions. Its form was not the form of a bird of the air, but it kept poising its long flight-feathers like polished oar-shafts. And soon after they heard the bitter cry Prometheus gave as his liver was torn away; and the air rang with his yells until they sighted the ravening eagle soaring back again from the mountain on the self-same track."

Not long after they came to the mouth of the River Phasis, and "on their left hand was the lofty Caucasus and the Cytæan city of Aea (Colchis), and on the other hand the plain of Ares and Ares' sacred grove, where the serpent kept watch and ward over the Fleece, hanging on the leafy branches of an oak." So the heroes anchored the "Argo" in a shady backwater, and there debated how they should achieve their end. Fortunately for them, Hera and Athene decided to come to their assistance, in a way we will tell later. The heroes' own idea was the extremely simple one of going up to the Court of the King Æetes and asking him to give them the Fleece. Jason was sent, and the king, on hearing the request, was filled with rage, and said, "Were it not that you had been guests at my table, verily I would have cut out your tongues and chopped off both hands and sped you forth with your feet alone." The king, being unable to do this, as they had broken bread with him, thought of a tremendous trial: "Two brazen-footed bulls are mine, that pasture on the Plain of Ares, and breathe forth flame from their jaws; them I yoke and drive over the stubborn field of Ares, four plough-gates; quickly I furrow it with the plough-share as far as the headland, casting into the furrows by way of seed, not the corn of Deme-

13

ter, but the teeth of a dreadful serpent which spring up into the fashion of armed men; them I slay at once, laying them low beneath my spear as they leap against me on every side. In the morning I yoke the oxen, and in the evening I cease from the harvest. And thou, if thou canst accomplish such deeds as these, on that very day thou shalt carry off the Fleece."

Jason was not cheered by the prospect, and "sat where he was, mute and helpless in a sorry plight." The time had come for Hera and Athene to help him. Their plan was to persuade Eros to "let fly his arrow at the daughter of Æetes (Medea) and bewitch her with love for Jason." As some of the most beautiful writing in the poem is concerned with the love-making of Jason and Medea, we will give a few details. Eros had passed into the palace with Jason, and Medea was watching his interview with her father, Æetes. Eros took the opportunity to quickly string his bow and fit an arrow from his quiver, and shoot at Medea. "Deep into the maiden's heart like a flame burnt his shaft; and ever she kept darting bright glances straight up at Æson's son, while inside her breast the heart panted quick in its anguish; all recollection left her, and with the sweet pain her very soul melted."

Poor Medea retired to her chamber, after she had heard the judgment of her father Æetes, and "in her soul much she pondered all the cares that the

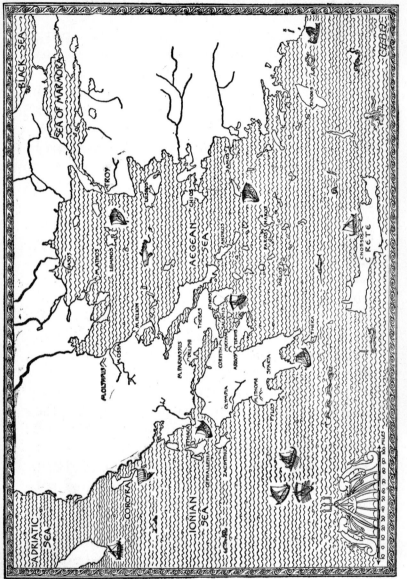

FIG. 6.—Map of Homeric Greece and the Surrounding Seas.

B.M.

Fig. 7.—The Minotaur.

Loves arouse. And before her eyes the vision still remained—the likeness of himself, how he was clad, such words as he spake, how he sat in his chair, how he went out towards the door—and, brooding, there never was such another man she thought; while always in her ears rang his voice and the honey-sweet words which he had uttered. And she feared for him." Was there ever such a dilemma for a poor maiden? Jason did not even know that she loved him, and how was she to tell him? Æetes wanted to kill Jason, and Medea very much wanted to keep him alive. Medea wanted to help Jason with her magic arts, because she was something of a sorceress, and yet that seemed very disloyal to her own father. In the end love won, of course, and a message was sent to Jason to meet her at the holy shrine of Hecate. There Medea waited for him, and when he came and spoke to her, "her soul melted within her, uplifted by his praise, and she gazed upon him face to face; nor did she know what word to utter first, but was eager to pour out everything at once." Even a dull male like Jason began to see what was in the wind, because we read a little later, "now both were abashed and fixed their eyes upon the ground, and again they glanced up at one another, smiling with the light of love beneath their radiant brows."

So Medea gave a charm to Jason which enabled him to carry out the hard task imposed by Æetes.

Then the Golden Fleece was seized by the Argonauts, and carried off, and with them went Medea, because she feared her father's wrath for helping Jason. Of their marriage, which was not happy, or the further travels of the Argonauts before they reached home, we cannot here tell, but they should be read in the translation of R. C. Seaton in the Loeb Library.

Modern scholars think that the "Voyage of the Argonauts" was a poetical description of the travels of men seeking the Land of Gold. The early miners first found gold by its sparkle in the beds of streams, then traced it to the rocks from which it had been washed out. Then they are supposed to have recovered the gold dust, which was being carried down stream, by suspending a fleece in the water so that the grains would be caught in the oily wool. When Jason snatched the Golden Fleece from the oak-grove, "from the shimmering of the flocks of wool there settled on his fair cheeks and brow a red flush like a flame."

Down through all the ages men have desired gold for the sheen of its beauty. A visit to the Prehistoric Room at the British Museum will show how much it was used here in England for ornaments in the Bronze Age. We refer to it in "E.L.," II., p. 126.[1] Only in our time is gold dug out of the earth in one part of the world, to be

[1] "Everyday Life" Series, by the same authors.

The Argonauts

buried in a vault in another; obviously because we fear its magical qualities.

The legendary history of the "Argo" will have helped us to understand the love of adventure and movement of the Greek people. The character of the country played a great part in their development. Like Norway, the fertile plains are cut off one from another by mountain ranges in between. This led to the founding of small city States, and genius flourishes better so than in the vast ant-heaps of modern man. When the inhabitants of these small States became too numerous to be supported by the surrounding countryside, like the Norsemen later on, they were forced to go to sea as sailors, traders, or pirates. Sailing about, they discovered other desirable places, and so founded colonies. The incomparable beauty of their country turned them into poets. The people lived on the plains, and their gods on the cloud-topped mountains.

A glance at the map of their world, Fig. 6, will show that Greece was well placed to play a part in classical times as a maritime nation. The Great Powers then were Egypt, Assyria, and Persia, and the trading ports in Asia Minor could easily be reached by Greek boats. Yet they were far enough away not to be a source of danger, unless the enemy understood the use of the sea; and they did not. When Persia did at last attack Greece, its navy was only used as an auxiliary to its army, which had to cross the Hellespont, and make the weary journey by land, through Macedonia and Thessaly. Greece was left to herself, free to grow, until she was strong enough to resist oppression.

Another great Power had to wax and wane before her time came. The Minoans, a Mediterranean people living in the island of Crete, had developed the wonderful civilisation which has been unearthed by Sir Arthur Evans in the palace at Cnossus.

Their greatest period seems to have been between 1650–1450 B.C., and then catastrophe fell upon them. They were another seafaring people, and built up their kingdom on trade. Their ships sailed to the Nile with oil and wine, wheel-made pottery and sponges, and they were known there as the Keftiu. The Minoans must have had some early connection with Greece. The legend of the Minotaur, a huge bull-like monster kept in a labyrinth at Cnossos, and fed on seven youths and seven maidens sent each year by the Athenians, is, in all probability, a poetical rendering of some less bloodthirsty tribute.

Our illustration, Fig. 7, from a sixth-century black figure vase, suggests that the wily Athenians picked out rather stringy youths and maidens, because the Minotaur looks thin and hungry and not huge.

Theseus, the great hero of the Greeks, went one

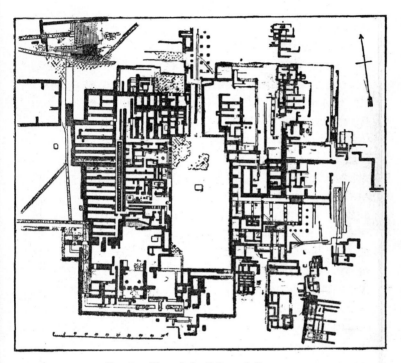

Fig. 8.—Plan of the Palace of Cnossos.

Fig. 9.—The Great Stairs at Cnossos.

The Argonauts

year, and Ariadne, the daughter of Minos, the King of Crete, fell in love with him. She provided Theseus with a sword to kill the Minotaur, and a thread to find his way out of the labyrinth. If you go to Cnossos to-day to see the ruins uncovered by the patient labour of Sir Arthur Evans, it is easy to see how the legend of the labyrinth may have grown up. The palace had a great central courtyard surrounded by a perfect maze of small chambers and winding passages in which any stranger must have lost his way.

Fig. 9 shows the great stairs leading down from the courtyard to the king's quarters. The characteristic Minoan columns with shafts tapering downwards should be noted.

Of course the palace, which was destroyed about 1450 B.C., was much later than the one of the legend of Theseus, but the legend is proof that in that earlier time Crete was great and powerful, and Greece had to depend on her heroes for protection. Theseus was a friend of the Argonauts. The palace was built in a pleasant valley, some few miles from the sea, and was not defended by any system of fortifications. The ruins to-day conjure up in one's mind a picture of all that one has ever imagined of Eastern palaces, and it is difficult to find any resemblance between the plan of Cnossos and the later fortified acropolis of the Greeks. But many of the Minoan details were transplanted, as we shall see. These details may have been learned from articles which were imported into Greece from Crete. The celebrated gold cups, found at Vaphio in Laconia, are undoubtedly of Minoan manufacture. They may have been bought in legitimate trade, but more probably they formed part of the loot of a raid, and for this reason. It is thought that about 1450 B.C., one of those movements of which we have written in our other books began. Northerners began to filter down into Greece, and to these men the name of Achæans has been given. The closest parallel would be those other Northmen, Norsemen, or Normans, who attacked the Franks and settled down in a part of Gaul, Normandy, in A.D. 912. We know that the Normans when they arrived were much like the people described in "Beowulf" (see "E.L.," IV.). They were not bent on destruction, but once secure in their new home were content to learn from the Franks how to build stone castles and wonderful cathedrals.

In much the same way it would seem that the Achæans did not destroy the Minoan influence on the mainland of Greece, but instead learned how to build from the work they found there. They used the inverted tapering columns, and other details of decoration, but the planning of the buildings was made to correspond to their particular needs, and, like the Normans, they wanted, not palaces,

but fortified castles. Here we might remind our
readers that, though we are writing of what happened over 3,300 years ago, that is only yesterday
so far as the history of the Mediterranean is concerned—Sir Arthur Evans found Neolithic, or New
Stone Age, remains under the buildings at Cnossos,
and it is probable that the Minoans were descended
from the same Mediterranean stock that found
their way to England in the New Stone Age, and
of whom we wrote in "E.L.," II.

We can now pass on to another name honoured
in archæology, that of Dr. Schliemann. We cannot here tell how, as a poor boy, he conceived the
idea of excavating Troy; of his struggles first to
educate himself, and then to escape from the trap
of commercialism, but in the end it was done, and
his life is one of the great romances, and an inspiration to all other boys not born with a silver
spoon for feeding purposes. During Schliemann's
youth and middle age, everything was subordi-
nated to this one purpose, and when at last his
dream came true, his excavations at Troy, Mycenæ, and Tiryns laid bare the background of a
life like that described in the Homeric poems.

Every detail of the poems is the subject of keen
debate by scholars all over the world, and their
debates can be Homeric in intensity. This only
means that the subject is so vitally interesting and
important that it rouses men. It would be imper-

tinent for us to enter the lists. All that we intend to do is to illustrate the details of the "Iliad" and the "Odyssey" as far as possible, by the discoveries of the archæologists. If our readers are interested, they can then become scholars themselves, and throw javelins barbed with words in the best company.

FIG. 10.—General View of the Site of the Palace of Cnossos from the South.

(*From a Photograph kindly lent by* Mr. THEODORE FYFE.)

FIG. 11.—Vaphio Cup.   (See p. 24.)

FIG. 12.—Nestor's Cup.   (See p. 51.)

(From the reproductions in the Gem Room at the British Museum.)

CHAPTER II

Book I.—The first book of the "Iliad" opens when the Greeks have been besieging Ilios or Troy for nine years. There is no dull setting of the scene, but we are at once plunged into the quarrel between Agamemnon and Achilles. Agamemnon had taken the daughter of Chryses, the priest, who prays without avail that she may be restored to him. Then Phœbus Apollo was wroth at heart, and the dread clanging of his bow was heard, and for nine days the gods' shafts ranged through the host. Agamemnon is persuaded to send back Chryseis to her father, but takes Briseis from Achilles, who is restrained by the goddess Athene from taking vengeance on Agamemnon.

As so often happened, the heroes had sprung from the immortals, and though the father of Achilles was Peleus, King of the Myrmidons, his mother was Thetis, a goddess of the sea. She, indignant at the slight put on her son, rose up from the waves, and went to the home of the gods

29

on many-ridged Olympus. There she spoke to
Zeus, son of Cronos, and father of the gods, and
prayed him to grant victory to the Trojans, until
the Greeks should honour her son Achilles. Zeus
is troubled, being a little afraid what ox-eyed Hera,
his wife, will say. She does upbraid him, and lame
Hephaistos, their son, tries to make peace, saying,
"Verily a sorry business this will be and not endur-
able, if ye two thus fall out for mortals' sake, and
bring dissension among the gods."

This is just what does happen in the "Iliad."
Not only do the mortals fight on earth, but the
gods descend from Olympus and take sides, and,
quarrelling between themselves, the whole heavens
become full of the thunder of their tremendous
combat.

There are many interesting details in this first
book. Odysseus, of many devices, takes back
Chryseis to her father, in a ship with twenty oarsmen, and a hecatomb of a hundred animals to be
sacrificed to the Far-darter Apollo. Arrived at
Chryse "they furled their sails and stowed them
in the black ship; the mast they lowered by the
forestays and quickly brought it to the crutch, and
rowed her with oars to the anchorage. Then they
flung out the anchor stones and made fast the
hawsers." Then follow details of the sacrifice to
Apollo. The animals are set in order around the
altar. The men wash their hands and take up the

barley meal. The priest prays to Apollo to stay his affliction of the Greeks, and sprinkles the barley meal. The animals' heads are drawn back, and they are slaughtered and flayed. Slices are cut from the thighs and wrapped in fat, making a double fold. Raw collops were laid thereon, and the priest "burnt them on billets of wood and poured libation over them of gleaming wine; and at his side the young men held five-pronged forks. Now, when the thighs were consumed and they had tasted of the vitals, then all the rest they carved up and spitted it and roasted it well, and took it off the fire again." Then they feasted, and after worshipped the god with music.

This ceremonial of the sacrifice followed by the feast was to remain until Christian times. Pope Gregory even recommended that the early Christians "no more offer beasts to the devil, but kill cattle to the praise of God in their eating" ("E.L.," IV., p. 93).

It should be noted that we have not yet been told why the Greeks had gone to besiege Troy. There is one reference in the quarrel between Achilles and Agamemnon, where Achilles says:—

> ". . . But it was thy lead we followed here, thou shameless one, for thy pleasure, to win thee thy due from the Trojans, thee and Menelaos, thou dog-face!"

Everyday Life in Homeric Greece

It was not necessary for Homer to tell his audience that Paris, or Alexandros, the son of the King of Troy, had stolen Helen of Argos, the wife of Menelaos, who was the brother of Agamemnon. The "Iliad," like our own Anglo-Saxon poem, "Beowulf," was a tale that had been told, and retold, a thousand times, until it was fixed into its final form by the genius of Homer. So the old Greeks would have found a great deal of their pleasure in the actual telling of the tale.

We must think of the "Iliad" as a tale well told by Homer, one of the world's great tale-tellers, and not only as a written book to be read.

Had Homer lived to-day he would have been a great broadcaster. He realised the necessity of interesting his listeners at the very beginning, hence the dramatic quality of the first book of the "Iliad," with the quarrel of Achilles and Agamemnon, which is to have such tragic consequences for the Greeks.

Book II.—In the second book we find how the Greeks are moved to renew their attack on the Trojans, and then follows a catalogue of the men and their ships. They had come from Athens and Argos, Tiryns of the great walls, from Corinth, Sparta, and Arcadia.

"Odysseus led the great-hearted Cephallenians, them that possessed Ithaca and Neriton with quivering leafage."

The "Iliad"

From all parts of Greece they came, and their great opponent was Hector of the glancing helm, the son of Priam, and leader of the Trojans.

Book III.—In the third book we find the Greeks and Trojans drawn up in battle array against one another. This did not mean that one smudge of men on one horizon fired at another smudge on the other, as they would do to-day. The Greeks and Trojans would not have been parted by much more than a bow-shot.

Then comes the challenge of Paris, who stole Helen, to all the chieftains of the Argives, to fight him man to man in deadly combat, and the challenge is taken up by Menelaos, the injured husband. Then Paris was daunted, and shrank back, until Hector his brother drove him to fight. It was then arranged that the two should fight, and the winner was to have Helen and all her wealth, and the war between the Greeks and Trojans was to cease. The men in the ranks of the Greeks and Trojans sat down. Lambs were brought for sacrifice, and Priam was sent for that he might pledge the oath. Helen was told that: "Alexandros and Menelaos, dear to the War-god, will contest thee with their long spears; thou shalt be proclaimed dear wife of him who conquers." The sacrifice was offered, then Paris gained the right to cast the first spear. "And upon his back fair Alexandros girt his splendid harness, Alexandros, spouse to Helen of the lovely hair. First of all upon his legs he donned his greaves, which were beautiful to see, and clasped with silver round the ankles. Then upon his breast he put the corselet of his brother Lykaon, settling it to fit him. Across his shoulders he threw his brazen sword, silver studded, taking as well a shield, huge and sturdy. Upon his mighty head he placed a strongly wrought helmet, topped with an awful plume of nodding horsehair, and picked a strong spear, easy to his hand. And thus, too, did warlike Menelaos gird on his harness. . . . " The fight is described, first Alexandros "flung his spear whose shadow flies afar; and it drove against Menelaos's round target, but its bronze point did not pierce the stout target, but turned back. . . ." Then Menelaos "lifted and hurled his spear and struck against the round target of Priam's son. Into the bright shield drove the heavy shaft, and on into the wrought corselet, until it had ripped the jerkin at his flank; but he plunged aside and so shunned black death. Then Menelaos drew his sword and, heaving up his arm, brought it down upon the other's helmet-ridge, but the steel shivered into three and four pieces, and dropped from his hand."

Then comes the typically Greek touch to the tale.

"Menelaos leapt upon Paris, and caught him by the horsehair crest of his helmet, and would have killed him, and gained again his wife Helen." But this would have been far too like plain sailing. Man would not have been shown as the sport of the gods, struggling along a difficult path, and only winning to his end, or losing all, through tragic happenings. Zeus's daughter, Aphrodite, comes to the assistance of Paris, and hurls him through thick darkness to safety in the palace of Priam. The Trojans were quite innocent of any wish to hide him from Menelaos, because "he was hated of all, even as black death."

The fates were against them all; they needs must fight, and from this there was no escape.

Book IV.—The fourth book opens with a consultation between the gods as to "whether once more we shall arouse ill war and the dread battle-din, or put friendship between the foes."

Father Zeus, who loves the men of holy Ilios (Troy), wishes for peace, but Athene and Hera sit by him, and devise ills for the Trojans. It is Hera who conceives the diabolical plan of making the Trojans break their oath, and do violence to the Greeks. Athene is sent in the likeness of a man, and persuades Pandaros to shoot an arrow at Menelaos. "Forthwith he unsheathed his polished bow of horn of wild ibex." Pandaros had shot the ibex himself, and taken the horns, sixteen palms in length, to a worker in horn, who joined them cunningly together and polished them all well, and set the tip of gold thereon. After the bow had been strung, Pandaros's comrades held their shields before him, and he took a feathered arrow and laid the bitter dart upon the string, and vowed to Apollo, the lord of archery, one hundred firstling lambs:-

". . . He drew his bow, holding in the same grasp the arrow-notch and the bow-string of ox's sinew, and stretched back the bow-string as far as his breast, and the iron arrow-head as far as the bow, and, when he had drawn the great bow into a circle, the bow twanged and the string hummed aloud and the sharp arrow sped forth, keen to wing its way into the press. . . ." The daughter of Zeus protected Menelaos, and turned the arrow aside from the flesh, so that "on the clasped belt it struck and drove through the rich belt and through the curious corselet, on through the metal-studded apron which he wore to guard his flesh against darts; and this it was defended him best, but this too did the arrow pierce, grazing his outermost flesh and straightway the dark blood poured from his wound. . . ." The taslet made by the coppersmith was worn beneath the corselet. Menelaos's legs were stained with blood, "just as when a Maionian or Karian woman stains ivory with scarlet to make the cheek-piece that horses wear." These ivory cheek-pieces for horses were used here in England (see "E.L.," II., Fig. 57).

Fig. 13.—Helen and Paris.

Fig. 14.—Hephaistos.

B.M.

Fig. 15.—Warriors.

The "Iliad"

The Greeks had army doctors, because Machaon, the hero son of Asklepios, the noble leech, is called in. He draws out the arrow from the wound, sucks out the blood, and cunningly spreads thereon soothing drugs.

This treachery, to which the Trojans were forced by the gods, leads to renewed battle between them and the Greeks. This is a point which must not be lost sight of. The combatants, like the men in our Great War, fought, not because they loved fighting, but because fate drove them on.

The method of fighting described by Homer is different from that of classical Greece. Nestor of the Pylians "first drew up the charioteers with their horses and their chariots, and behind them the infantry many and brave, to be a bulwark in fight. The cowards he thrust into the middle, that, however backward a man might be, willy-nilly they must all do battle. And to the charioteers first he gave their orders, bidding them hold in their horses, and see to it that they did not become entangled in the press. 'Nor do any of you,' he said, 'because he trusts in his skill with horses and in his valour, hanker after fighting the Trojans alone in front of the rest, nor yet draw back behind his fellows. So will your force be diminished. But, when a man from his own chariot can come at the chariot of a foeman, then let him drive in his spear; thus it is best.' Thus, too, did men of olden times

39

lay low cities and ramparts, having such counsel as this. . . ."

The men fought with spear and sword, or cast stones at one another, and protected themselves with bucklers. It is difficult to discover any method in the fighting in the pages of Homer, because he lays stress on a series of combats between champions of either side, sometimes on foot and sometimes in their chariots. Only, "Achilles, son of fair-haired Thetis, fights not, but among the ships nurses his bitter rage."

Book V.—In the fifth book Diomedes is helped by Pallas Athene to distinguish between god and man, but warned that ". . . if any god comes here to try thee, fight thou not face to face with any other immortal, but only Aphrodite, daughter of Zeus—if she should enter the battle, let drive at her with the sharp bronze."

Diomedes attacked the Trojans with fury, and came near to killing Aineias, whose mother was Aphrodite. She came to her son's assistance, only to be wounded herself by Diomedes. "Then started forth the blood of the immortal goddess, ichor, such as flows in the veins of the blessed gods; bread they do not eat, nor do they drink gleaming wine, wherefore are they bloodless and are called immortals. So, with a loud cry, she let fall her son; and him Phœbus Apollo lifted in his arms and sheltered him in a dark cloud."

40

The "Iliad"

Aphrodite escapes to Olympus, and there stirs up Ares, blood-stained bane of mortals, to encourage the Trojans to fresh effort, which meets with such success that Hera comes to the assistance of the Greeks with her daughter Athene. "Then, Hera, the goddess queen, daughter of great Cronos, busied herself harnessing the horses with their golden frontlets, and Hebe swiftly put to the car, on either side, its curved brazen wheels, eight-spoked, fitted upon iron axle-trees; of these the felloe is wrought in imperishable gold, and over them are bronze tyres, a marvel to see; the naves are silver, which revolve on this side and on that; the body of the car is woven tight, with plait-work of gold and silver thongs and rimmed about with two rails. From the body stood out a silver pole, upon the end of which she fastened the splendid golden yoke, throwing over it the golden breast-straps. And beneath the yoke Hera led the fleet-footed horses; and she longed for the battle and the sound of the war-cry. And Athene, daughter of Zeus who bears the ægis, slipped off, upon the floor of her father's house, her fine, many-coloured robe that her own hands had woven, putting on, instead, the tunic of cloud-gathering Zeus, and donned her armour for woeful strife. About her shoulders she cast the terrible tasselled ægis. Panic is set all about it like a crown, and Discord is therein, and Valour, Onset too, that makes the blood run cold, and therein is the Gorgon's head (Medusa, killed by Perseus), that dreadful monster, awful and grim, a portent of Zeus who bears the ægis. Upon her head she placed the golden helmet, two-horned and set with bosses four, decked with the men-at-arms of a hundred cities. Into the flaming chariot then she stepped, and grasped her spear, heavy and huge and stout, with which she vanquishes the ranks of men, of heroes, even, against whom she is wroth, Athene, daughter of the awful sire."

They go to Olympus, and ask Father Zeus if they may "smite Ares and drive him from the battle in sorry plight." They obtain his permission, and then seek Diomedes on the battle-field. The Greeks have had to give ground to the Trojans, who have been helped by Ares. Athene mounts a chariot by the side of Diomedes, and the goddess drives it against Ares, and Diomedes with her assistance wounds him with his spear. "Then brazen Ares bellowed out loud as nine thousand warriors, or as ten thousand, shouting in battle, when they mingle in the War-god's strife. And trembling came upon Achæans and Trojans alike; fear took hold of them; so mighty was the bellowing of Ares, the greedy of battle." This is an extraordinary thing, that Homer could have thought of a god as so human that he bellows out loud when he is wounded.

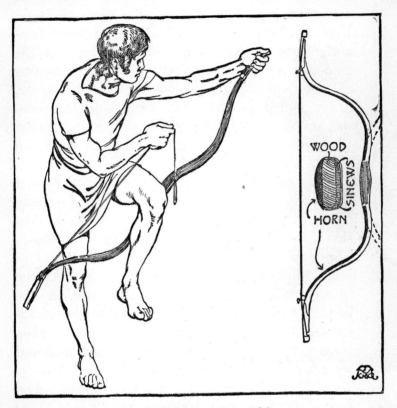

WOOD

SINEWS

HORN

Fig. 16.—The Back-Bent Bow of Odysseus.

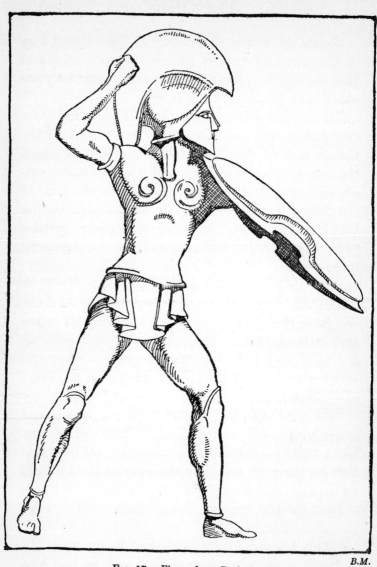

Fig. 17.—Figure from Dodona.

So, in the words of the "Iliad," the dread fray of Trojans and Greeks swayed oft this way and that across the plain, as they aimed against each other their bronze-shod javelins.

To us, as a work of art, the "Iliad" presents a tremendous picture of war and strife; but to the Greek, and to the Greek child of classical times, the effect of hearing it spoken with dramatic emphasis must have been terrific. To us the gods of the "Iliad" are the gods of mythology; to the Greeks, Athene was the goddess to whom Pericles caused the Parthenon to be built on the Acropolis in Athens.

Book VI.—In book six Hector goes to Troy, to ask his mother to vow to sacrifice to Athene, if she will have mercy on the city and the Trojans' wives and little children. There he meets Andromache, his wife, and then follows the pathetic scene in which they lament the fate which threatens Troy. She reminds him:

". . . No, Hector, to me thou art father and queenly mother; brother thou art and valiant husband besides. Come now, take pity on me; stay here on the wall, lest thou shouldst make thy child an orphan, and a widow me thy wife."

But Hector cannot shrink from battle, even though as he says:

"This I know in my heart and in my soul: the day will come when sacred Ilios will be laid low, and Priam, and his people who wield the good ash spear . . ." and Andromache would be led captive by the Greeks. Then Hector cries:

"But dead may I be and the heaped-up earth covering me, before I hear thy cries as they carry thee away into bondage."

Book VII.—In the seventh book Apollo and Athene stay the general battle, and Apollo suggests:

". . . Let us stir up the valiant spirit of Hector, tamer-of-horses, that perchance he may challenge some one of the Danaans, in single fight, to encounter him man to man in deadly combat."

The warriors are given a rest, "and Athene and Apollo of the silver bow settled upon the tall oak tree of Father Zeus, who bears the ægis, in the shape of twin vultures, rejoicing in the warriors, where they sat together, packed close, bristling with shields and helms and spears."

The Greeks cast lots, and Aias in this way becomes their champion, and goes to meet Hector, "carrying his shield that was like a city-wall, a brazen shield, with sevenfold bull's-hide skilfully wrought him by Tychios—Tychios far best of all the workers in hide, who dwelt at Hyle, and had made him his flashing shield, of seven hides of mighty bulls and over them an eighth layer of bronze."

Then follows a long description of the fight, and as neither is able to kill the other, they exchange

46

gifts instead. This sounds extraordinary, until we remember that much the same kind of thing is written about in the pages of our own fourteenth-century Froissart. In both periods fighting was regarded as the riskiest of the sports.

As the general fighting was not renewed, the opportunity was taken to "assemble and carry hither the dead bodies on carts, with oxen and with mules; a little way distant from the ships will we burn them, so that every man, whensoever we return to our native land, may bear their bones home to their children; about the pyre let us raise one single barrow, rearing it from the plain for all of them in common; and thereby, with such speed as may be, let us build ourselves a lofty wall, as defence for us and for our ships. And in the midst thereof let us contrive close-shutting gates that they may afford a passage for chariots; and without let us dig a deep ditch close by, which shall intervene and hold off chariots and infantry, if ever we should be hard put to it by the onslaught of the lordly Trojans."

It seems rather late in the day for the Greeks to have fortified their camp. Their usual practice was to pull their ships up, and then protect them on the land side by a palisade. In this chapter we find them importing their supplies. Wine came from Lemnos, "and the long-haired Achæans brought them wine, some for bronze, some for gleaming iron, some for hides, some for whole cattle, and some for bond-slaves."

Fresh attempts at peace were made, this time by the Trojans, but Paris, who is the villain, refuses to give up Helen.

Book VIII.—In the eighth book the fight is renewed, but it must be remembered that all this time Achilles had not been fighting because of the wrong done him by Agamemnon. The gods still remember the plea of Thetis, the mother of Achilles, that the Trojans were to be victorious, until the Greeks should do honour to her son.

". . . Then the father lifted his golden balances, setting in the scales twin fates of grievous death, one for the horse-taming Trojans and one for the bronze-mailed Achæans; and, taking the scale-yard by the midst, he raised it, and the Achæans' day of doom sank down."

At the end of the book the Greeks are driven back within the walls of their camp by the ships.

Book IX.—The ninth book finds the Greeks dispirited, and Agamemnon tries to make friends with Achilles. He offers him ". . . seven tripods that fire has never touched, and ten talents of gold, and twenty shining cauldrons, and twelve strong horses, whose swiftness has won prizes in the race." He even offers to return the daughter of Briseus. Odysseus, of many wiles, is sent to make the offer to Achilles, who rejects it, saying:

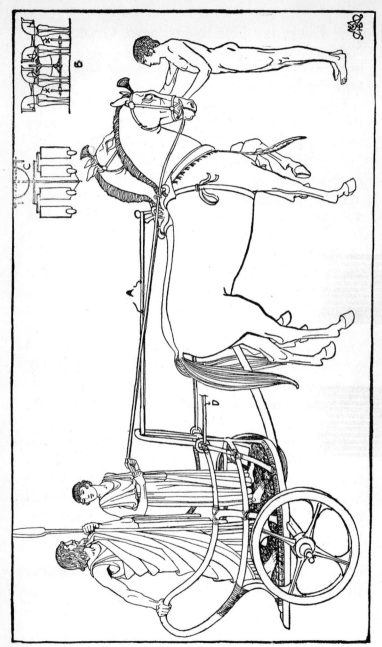

Fig. 18.—Chariot. (Reconstruction.)

Fig. 19.—Face of Gorgon—Corinthian, *c.* 570 B.C.

"His gifts are hateful to me, and himself I hold not worth a straw."

Book X.—The tenth book recounts the adventures of Odysseus and Diomedes, who go at night as spies to the camp of the Trojans.

Book XI.—In the eleventh book Agamemnon, Diomedes, and Odysseus are all wounded. Now we begin to hear more of Patroklos, the friend of Achilles. He is sent to inquire how it is that Nestor was borne out of the fight. Arrived at the hut, he finds that Hekamede has mixed for them a mess. ". . . First she drew before the two of them a fair, well-polished table with feet of cyanus, setting on it a vessel of bronze, with onion, as a relish to their drink, and pale honey and meal of sacred barley; and at their side a splendid cup that the old man had brought with him from home; embossed with golden studs it was, and there were four handles, and about each pair of handles were doves feeding, and below the cup stood upon two feet. Another man would scarce have found the strength to raise that cup from the table, when it was full, but old Nestor could lift it easily enough. In this cup the woman, like to the goddesses, mixed a potion for them with Pramnian wine, grating into it, with a brazen grater, goat's milk cheese, and sprinkling in white barley meal; and when she had prepared the potion she bade them drink."

Book XII.—In the twelfth book the Trojans besiege the Greeks in their camp, and in the end break down the walls and drive them to their ships.

Book XIII.—In the thirteenth book Poseidon, the god of the seas, goes to the assistance of the Greeks, and the fight continues among the ships.

Book XIV.—In the fourteenth book things continue to go so badly with the Greeks that Agamemnon suggests launching the first line of ships, and mooring them with stones so as to be able to escape. He is strongly rebuked by Odysseus. Poseidon again stirs up the Greeks to the attack, and Zeus is beguiled to sleep by Hera. The Greeks drive the Trojans from the camp, and Hector is wounded.

Book XV.—In the fifteenth book Zeus awakes from his sleep, and is angry to find that Hector has been wounded. He sends Iris as messenger to Poseidon, that he must cease helping the Greeks, and return to the sea. Apollo is sent to encourage Hector, and the Trojans carry the fight back to the ships, and throw fire at that belonging to Protesilaos.

Book XVI.—In the sixteenth book Patroklos beseeches Achilles to come to the assistance of the Greeks, and when he refuses, asks to be allowed to lead the Myrmidons himself. He borrows the armour of Achilles, and fights so well that he pushes the Trojans back to the walls of Troy. In the end Patroklos is killed by Hector. This, as we shall see, is the turning-point of the story.

The "Iliad"

Book XVII.—In the seventeenth book the fight rages round the body of Patroklos, whose armour, borrowed from Achilles, is stripped off by Hector.

Book XVIII.—In the eighteenth book Achilles hears of the death of his comrade: ". . . and in both his hands he scooped up black dust, and poured it on his head and fouled his comely face; and down on his sweet-scented jerkin rained the dark ashes. And there, in his mightiness, he lay outstretched in the dust, and, with his own hand, he tore and despoiled his hair. . . ."

His mother Thetis comes to comfort him, and promises to bring him new armour in the morning. Meanwhile, without armour, he encourages the Greeks, and helps them to bring back the body of Patroklos. The body is washed. ". . . Noble Achilles bade his comrades set a great cauldron on the fire that, as soon as might be, they should wash from Patroklos's body the bloody gore. And on the blazing fire they put the cauldron for filling the bath, pouring in water and taking wood and kindling it beneath. Then round the belly of the cauldron played the flames and the water grew hot. And when the water was boiling within the bright bronze, then did they wash his body, anointing him richly with oil, salving his wounds with rare ointment; and they laid him on his bed, and from head to foot swathed him in a soft linen cloth and, above that, in a white robe. Then, all night long, round swift-footed Achilles, the Myrmidons bewailed and lamented Patroklos."

Thetis goes to Hephaistos, the lame god, to ask him to make new armour for Achilles, and Hephaistos ". . . went to his bellows and, turning them towards the fire, bade them work. Then the bellows, that numbered twenty in all, blew upon the melting-vats, or pots, sending forth deft blasts of variable strength, now to further his labour, and now again however Hephaistos might will it, according as his work went on. And on to the fire he threw tough bronze and tin and precious gold and silver."

If reference is made to "E.L.," II., p. 108, it will be found that bronze was smelted here in England in the Bronze Age in just the same way. Hephaistos first fashioned "a shield huge and strong, adorning it cunningly all over, circling it with a shining rim, threefold and glittering, and hung from it a baldric of silver. With five layers was covered the shield itself; and into it he put much cunning workmanship, with his curious skill." It was decorated with emblems of the earth, the heavens, the sun, moon, and stars, and fair cities of mortal men, and beautiful pictures of country life. These should be studied either in the original, or the translations we mention in our list of authorities. Homer is evidently telling of scenes with which he was familiar. You read of the hinds

B.M.

Fig. 20.—Casting lots before Athene.

Fig. 21.—Merchant Ship.

reaping with sharp sickles, and the sheaf binders following with twisted bands of straw, while others beneath an oak made ready a feast. Then we hear of the vintage, and a boy making pleasant music while the grapes are gathered. Again of a dancing place, and a great company standing around the lovely dance in joy. Hephaistos was right when he promised Thetis that, though he could not ward off dolorous death from Achilles, his armour should be the marvel of all men.

Book XIX.—The nineteenth book opens with the reconciliation between Agamemnon and Achilles. Only a day has passed since Odysseus first went to the hut of Achilles with the offer of peace, and now the gifts are accepted, and Briseis goes back. Achilles puts on his armour—greaves for his legs, with silver ankle-pieces, and a cuirass round his breast. A silver-studded bronze sword hung from his shoulder, and the great shield to ward off blows. A stout helmet with a horse-hair crest covered his head, and in his hand he carried his father's spear. So armed, Achilles joins in the fight, and plays havoc with the Trojans, and this is told in the twentieth book.

Book XX.—Zeus calls the gods to council. He determines to remain within a fold of Olympus himself, where he can gladden his heart with gazing at the battle, but gives the other gods permission to help whom they will.

Everyday Life in Homeric Greece

". . . So spake the son of Cronos and roused implacable war. And the gods went forth to the battle, some on this side and some on that: to the ships went Hera, and in her company Pallas Athene, and Earth-shaking Poseidon, and Hermes the Helper, who excelled them all in his subtlety; with them too went Hephaistos, in the pride of his great strength, limping, but under him his spindle legs moved nimbly. To the Trojans went Ares of the glancing helmet, and with him Phœbus the unshorn, and Artemis the Archer, and Leto and Xanthos and Aphrodite the laughter-loving."

Thus we have the amazing spectacle of not only men, but the actual gods warring between themselves.

Book XXI.—In the twenty-first book Achilles captures twelve young men alive, and binding them with thongs, sends them back to the Greek ships. In this chapter Achilles fights with the River Xanthos. We must remember that to the Greeks a river could be a god, to be propitiated by sacrifice.

"Nor shall the river avail you anything, fair-flowing with its silver eddies, though long time have you made him sacrifice of many bulls, and thrown down single-hooved horses, still living, into his eddies."

This river in the "Iliad" is something so alive that it can call on Apollo to help it against Achilles: "Just as when a man from its dark spring leads

forth a stream of water along a channel amid his
crops and garden, and, a mattock in his hand,
clears all hindrances from its path; and, as it flows,
it sweeps the pebbles before it, and, murmuring,
swiftly on it slides, down a sloping place, and out-
strips even him who leads it; so did the river-flood
overtake Achilles, make what speed he could; for
the gods are mightier than men." And the river
comes near to drowning Achilles, until Hephaistos
comes to his assistance, with a great fire that
parches the plain and stays the water. After, the
Greeks, with the assistance of Achilles, drive the
Trojans in flight within the walls of Troy.

Book XXII.—In the twenty-second book Hector
is shown outside the walls awaiting the onslaught
of Achilles. He reproaches himself because he did
not take the advice of Polydamas, who had suggested that they should retire within the walls of
Troy when they first heard that Achilles was to
take the field again. Hector flees from Achilles:
"And so, with flying feet, did these two thrice make
the circle of Priam's city; and all the gods gazed
down on them." And always Achilles headed him
off towards the plain, and prevented Hector from
running under the walls to gain the help of the
archers on the battlements. ". . . But when a
fourth time they had reached the springs, then the
father lifted up his golden balances, and in them
set two fates of gloomy death, one for Achilles and

one for horse-taming Hector, grasping the balance at the midpoint and poising it. Then down sank Hector's dooms-day and descended into the house of Hades; and Phœbus Apollo deserted him."

Athene, by a base trick, urges Hector to the fight, and he is killed by Achilles, who ". . . contrived a shameful treatment for goodly Hector, slitting behind the tendons of both his feet from the heel up to the ankle, threading through ox-hide thongs binding them to the chariot and leaving the head to trail. Then he mounted his chariot and, after he had lifted in with him the famous armour, he lashed up his horses and they sprang forward with a will. And about Hector, as they dragged him along, rose the dust, his dark locks streaming loose on either side; and now in the dust lay that head once so fair, for Zeus had given him over to his enemies, to suffer shameful treatment in his own native land."

Of the lament of Andromache we cannot write, and of how, when "she gained the wall and the throng of men who stood there, and, standing still, she looked and saw him where he was being dragged before the city; ruthlessly were the swift horses dragging him away towards the hollow ships of the Achæans. Then the darkness of night settled down over her eyes and wrapped her about, and she reeled backwards and panted forth her spirit."

Book XXIII.—In the twenty-third book the

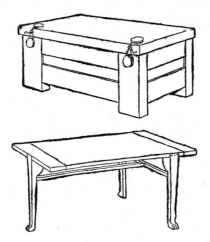

Fig. 22.—Chest and Table.

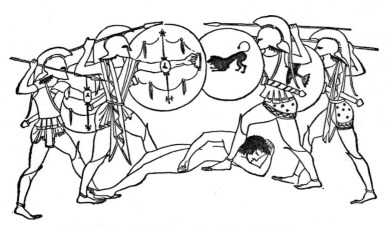

Fig. 23.—The fight over the body of Patroklos.

B.M.

Fig. 24.—Gathering Olives.

funeral feast of Patroklos is described. Oxen, sheep, goats, and boars were sacrificed. At night the spirit of Patroklos appears to his friend.

"Thou sleepest and has forgotten me, Achilles. While I lived never didst thou forget me, and only now that I am dead. Bury me with all despatch, so I may pass the gate of Hades. Far do the spirits keep me off, the spirits of men out-worn; they suffer not that I should join their company beyond the River; and vain are my wanderings through the wide-gated house of Hades. Pitifully I beg that thou shouldst give me thy hand; never again shall I come back from Hades, once you have granted me my due of fire."

In the morning ". . . Lord Agamemnon despatched men from all the huts with mules, to gather firewood." This was brought down to the shore and laid in great piles. The Myrmidons then armed themselves, the men in chariots going first and the footmen following, and in the midst was the body of Patroklos, borne by his comrades, who had cut off their hair, and heaped it on the body. A great pyre was made of wood. Then sheep and oxen were sacrificed, and the corpse of Patroklos was wrapped from head to foot in the fat taken from their bodies, and then placed on the pyre, the flayed bodies of the animals around it. Two-handled jars of honey and oil were added, and four strong-necked horses and two house-dogs.

Then the twelve unfortunate Trojan youths captured alive by Achilles, were killed, and their bodies went to swell the pile. All night long the pyre burned, and in the morning Achilles called on the chiefs of the Greeks to "first quench the burning of the pyre with wine, even so far as the might of the flames has reached; then let us gather up the bones of Patroklos, Menoitios's son, taking good care to single them out from the rest; easy they are to discern, since he lay in the middle of the pyre and the others upon its verge, apart, huddled together, horses and men. His bones let us place in a golden urn, and wrap them in a double fold of fat, till I too be hidden in Hades. No monstrous barrow do I ask that you should labour to raise— a decent barrow, no more; afterwards, you may raise it broad and high, such of you as may remain among the benched ships when I am gone."

Scenes such as this must have been enacted, and barrows raised, here in England in our own Bronze Age. [1]

Then follows an account of the funeral games: "Achilles checked the people where they stood; he made them sit down in a wide company, from his ships bringing out prizes—cauldrons and tripods, horses and mules and strong oxen, and fair-girdled women and grey iron.

"For swift chariot-racers first he awarded a

[1] See "E.L.," II., p. 135-8.

splendid prize—a woman skilful at fair handiwork for the winner to lead home, as well as an eared tripod that would hold twenty-two measures; so much for the first; for the second he awarded a six-year-old mare, unbroken; for the third a splendid cauldron untouched by fire, bright even as when it was first made; for the fourth two talents of gold; and for the fifth a two-handled urn that the fire had never scathed."

The winner of the boxing match obtained a sturdy mule, and the loser a two-handled cup. For wrestling, the first prize was a great tripod for standing on the fire, but curiously enough for the loser, Achilles ". . . led a woman into the midst, one skilled in many crafts, and whose worth they valued at four oxen." The wrestlers were Aias, son of Telamon, and Odysseus, and as neither could obtain the advantage, they were told to take equal prizes, and we do not know who got the four oxen's worth of femininity.

For the running races a mixing bowl of silver from Sidon, an ox, great and very fat, and half a talent of gold.

Book XXIV.—In the last book Priam comes to Achilles, and ransoms the body of Hector. Achilles promises to hold back the battle for twelve days, whilst the funeral ceremonies of Hector are being carried on.

Priam, helped by Hermes, brings back Hector's

body to Troy, and the people make lamentations. It is here that we come to the passage which moved Arthur to tears in "Tom Brown's School Days," when Helen says:—

"Thou would'st allay their anger with thy words, and restrain them by the gentleness of thy spirit and by thy gentle speech."

Then the body of Hector was burned as was that of Patroklos. "But when the young dawn shone forth, rosy-fingered Morning, then gathered the people round glorious Hector's pyre. Assembling, they first of all quenched the flames of the pyre with wine, even as far as the might of the flames had reached, and thereupon his brethren and friends gathered his white bones, mourning him with big tears coursing down their cheeks. The bones they took and laid away in a golden urn, wrapping them up in soft purple robes, and quickly set the urn in a hollow grave, and heaped above great stones, closely placed. Then hastily they piled a barrow, while everywhere about watchers were posted, through fear that the well-greaved Achæans might make an onslaught before the time. And, when the barrow was piled, they went back and, assembling, duly feasted and well in the palace of Priam, that king fostered by Zeus. Thus did they hold funeral for Hector, tamer of horses."

And that is the end of the "Iliad," and the Trojan, like all other wars, had a very sad end.

B.M.

Fig. 25.—Race of Warriors.

B.M.

Fig. 26.—Wrestling.

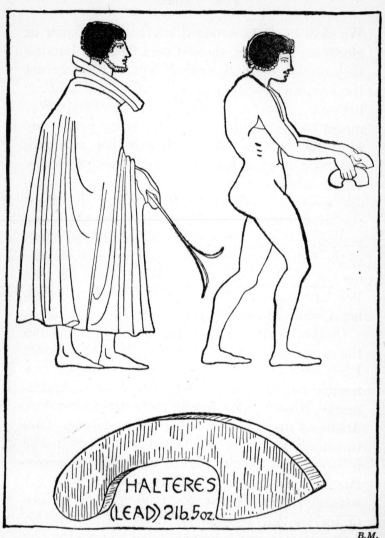

B.M.

Fig. 27.—Jumper holding lead jumping weights.

The " Iliad "

We shall be quite wrong if we think of Homer as glorifying war. He showed men fighting, because they needs must fight against fate. The gods cast the lots, and the men had to fight, and fighting, behaved as heroes. Consider what the Trojan War meant to the Greeks. For long weary years they were exiled from home, and how few returned. Agamemnon their king was one, but he took the virgin priestess Cassandra with him as a slave, and went to his death at the hands of Ægisthus, the lover of his own wife Clytemnestra. Odysseus, perhaps because of his share in urging the death of the babe, Astyanax, was condemned to wander for yet another ten years before he saw his wife Penelope again, and his mother died of a broken heart while he was away.

On the Trojan side the men were slaughtered and the women taken into slavery by the Greeks. Euripides's tragedy, "The Trojan Women," is a terrible picture of the aftermath of war. Andromache, Hector's wife, has been allotted to Pyrrhus, Achilles's son, and Hecuba, Hector's mother, tries to console her. She points out that Andromache is sweet and gentle, and if she tries to please Pyrrhus, perhaps he in his turn will be kind to her son Astyanax. The Greeks, however, had no idea of leaving Astyanax to grow up and avenge his father Hector, and a herald is sent to take the boy away and cast him from the walls. The scene

which follows is described by Professor Gilbert
Murray as "perhaps the most absolutely heart-
rending in all the tragic literature of the world."

> "Quick! take him; drag him; cast him from the wall,
> If cast ye will! Tear him, ye beasts, be swift!
> God hath undone me, and I cannot lift
> One hand, one hand, to save my child from death . . .
> O, hide my head for shame: fling me beneath
> Your galley's benches!"
>
> *Professor Gilbert Murray's Translation.*

Andromache is led away captive, and the dead boy
is brought back to his grandmother Hecuba, who
places him in Hector's shield and mourns over him.

Euripides may have been affected by the happenings of his own time. Another disgraceful massacre
had taken place when the Athenians killed all the
men of Melos and enslaved the women. This was
in 416 B.C. In 415 the disastrous expedition to
Syracuse set sail. Athens was in the hands of a
war party bent on creating an Empire. The
"Trojan Women" was produced just before the
expedition sailed, and must have been meant to
sound a note of warning.

CHAPTER III

THE "ODYSSEY"

Book I.—If we wish to find out what happened after the siege of Troy we must turn to the "Odyssey" of Homer, which is concerned with the travels of Odysseus. It is interesting to note that, just as in the "Iliad" our attention was at once riveted by an account of the quarrel between Achilles and Agamemnon, so in the "Odyssey" the first chapter gives an outline of the good things which are in store for us. We hear that Odysseus is held captive by the nymph Calypso in her hollow caves; that all the gods pity him, except Poseidon, who is angered with Odysseus because he blinded his son Polyphemus, one of the Cyclopes and a cannibal giant. The whole story really hinges on this quarrel.

The goddess Athene intercedes with Father Zeus on behalf of Odysseus, and Hermes is dispatched to Calypso, to tell her that Odysseus is to be released and sped on his way. Athene herself goes to Ithaca, the home of Odysseus, and "in the semblance of a stranger," introduces herself to Telemachus, the son of Odysseus. From him the goddess learns how the wealth of Odysseus is being wasted by many princes who, thinking that Odysseus, is dead, are wooing his wife Penelope. These wooers are the villains of the piece.

Athene recommends that Telemachus should fit out a ship and go to make inquiries of Nestor and Menelaos, who were at the siege of Troy with Odysseus, to see if by chance they have news of him, and the goddess plants courage in the heart of Telemachus. He tells the wooers that they must leave his halls.

Book II.—In book two Telemachus calls an assembly of the Achæans (the first since the departure of Odysseus), and the staff being placed in his hand, tells them of the misdeeds of the wooers. But Antinous, who was one of them, made answer that the fault was Penelope's, who gave hope to all, that now Odysseus was dead she would wed one of them when she had woven a shroud for Laertes, his father. "And this craft she planned in her heart, too; she set up in her halls a great web, fine-threaded and very broad, whereat she wove. . . . " Then at night Penelope unravelled her day's work, "and so for three whole years she hid it from the Achæans by her craft, and thus beguiled them."

The wooers tell the assembly that until Penelope

Fig. 28.—Hermes and Satyr.

FIG. 29.—Death of Ægisthus.

makes up her mind, they will remain in the house of Telemachus, and they continue to waste his substance in riotous feastings.

Telemachus makes ready for his voyage to Sparta and sandy Pylos. He goes to the treasure chamber ". . . where lay heaps of gold and bronze, and raiment in chests, and a good stock of fragrant olive oil. And there stood jars of wine, old and sweet, which held a divine, unmixed drink."

He tells the guardian to: ". . . draw me wine in jars, sweet wine and the choicest after that which thou art keeping against the return of that hapless one, if ever he come home again I know not whence, even Zeus-born Odysseus, having shunned death and the fates. Twelve jars fill and close them all with lids, and pour me barley-meal into well-sewn skins; let there be twenty measures of ground barley-meal."

Telemachus and the crew carry all on board, and Athene sends them a favourable wind.

"And when they had reared the fir-wood mast, they set it in its socket-hole and made it fast with the forestays, and with thongs of ox-hide hoisted the white sail. So the wind filled the belly of the sail, and the dark wave surged loudly about the stem of the flying ship."

Book III.—In book three, Athene, in the guise of Mentor, and Telemachus arrive at Pylos, and find Nestor and his people there on the seashore

sacrificing to Poseidon. Telemachus appeals to
Nestor for news of his father Odysseus, but Nestor
can only tell him how the return of the Achæans,
after the sack of Troy, was spoiled by dissensions,
some going one way, and some by others. He tells
the tale, which has become part of Greek literature,
how Agamemnon returned to find that his wife had
a lover, Ægisthus, by whom he was slain, and who
reigned in Mycenæ for seven years until he in turn
was killed by Orestes, the son of Agamemnon. The
tale of Nestor shows how much the Greeks were
at the mercy of the sea in their ships. With their
one square sail they could only sail with the wind,
and like Othere, the friend of our own King Alfred,
had to wait until that wind was favourable.[1] If
the wind became an unfavourable gale, they toiled
at their oars, and when their strength failed were
blown out of their course. This is what happened
to the Achæans returning from Troy.

Book IV.—In the fourth book Telemachus and
Peisistratus arrive by chariot in Sparta at the house
of Menelaos. This is how they were received:

"And the sweating horses they loosed from under
the yoke, and, tethering them at the horses' stalls,
they threw before them spelt, mixing in with it
white barley. The chariot they tilted up against
the shining walls of the entry, and led the men
away into the divine palace hall." After they had

[1] See "E.L.," IV., p. 131–2.

seen the palace, "they went to the polished baths
and bathed them." Then ". . . they sat down
on chairs beside Menelaos, Atreus's son. Then a
maid-servant brought water for their hands in a
golden pitcher and poured it over a silver basin, so
they might wash, drawing up at their side a polished table. And a sober housewife brought and
set by them bread, and dainties too in abundance,
giving them freely of her store. And a carver
lifted and put by them platters of all kinds of meat,
and near them he set two golden bowls."

Menelaos, as a sign of honour, gave them some
of his own dish of fat ox-chine roasted. All this
time they are entertained as strangers by Menelaos,
who, however, has been struck by the resemblance
of Telemachus to his friend Odysseus.

Then Helen, for whom the Achæans fought at
Troy, comes in, and she too marks the likeness.

She tells Telemachus tales of his father, of how,
at the siege of Troy, he disguised himself as a beggar
and passed into the Trojan city as a spy. Menelaos tells here:

"Never yet have mine eyes beheld such another
man as was steadfast-hearted Odysseus, no such
another deed as he planned and dared, in the carven
horse, wherein sat all we chiefs of the Argives,
carrying to the Trojans death and doom." And
how Helen came and "three times did'st thou circle
round the hollow ambush and try it with thy hands,

Everyday Life in Homeric Greece

calling aloud by name on the chiefs of the Argives, and with thy voice mimicking the voices of the wives of all the Danaans. Now I and Tydeus's son and goodly Odysseus were sitting in the midst; we heard thee call, and the two of us were anxious to rise and come forth, or straightway answer thee from within. Yet, for all our eagerness, Odysseus held us back and kept us there. Then, likewise, did the other sons of the Achæans keep silence; only Anticlus would have answered; but Odysseus shut his mouth with his strong hands and so saved all the Achæans, holding him thus till Pallas Athene led thee away again."

Telemachus then asks that he may be allowed to sleep, ". . . and Argive Helen ordered her maids that they should set bedsteads beneath the gallery of the entrance, and should lay on them fair purple blankets and above these spread coverlets, and thereover fleecy cloaks as a topmost covering of all. So, torch in hand, the maids went out of the hall and laid the bedding, and a serving man led forth the guests. So there they slept in the forehall of the house, noble Telemachus and Nestor's glorious son; but the son of Atreus slept in the inmost chamber of the high-roofed house, and at his side lay Helen of the long robes, that goddess among women."

In the morning, Menelaos tells Telemachus of how, in his own eight years' wandering, he heard

FIG. 30. — Raft of Odysseus. (Reconstruction.)

B.M.

Fig. 31.—Ball Game.

B.M.

Fig. 32.—Dancer.

The "Odyssey"

from Proteus, the thrall of Poseidon, how Odysseus was held captive by Calypso. Beyond that he cannot tell Telemachus anything.

Meantime the wooers ". . . in front of the palace of Odysseus took their pleasure in throwing the discus and the javelin, upon a levelled place, as was their custom, in the insolence of their pride."

They also laid their plans to kill Telemachus on his return from Pylos, and dispatched a ship to wait in the strait between Ithaca and Samos. The details of the return journey are given in the fifteenth book.

Book V.—In the fifth book Athene goes to the gods, who are in council, and asks Zeus that Calypso should free Odysseus. Hermes is sent to her with a message that she is to do so. Calypso must needs obey Zeus, but bewails the hard lot of goddesses who fall in love with mortals:

"Harsh are ye gods and jealous above all others, who grudge that goddesses should openly mate themselves to mortal men."

She points out how she had saved Odysseus from shipwreck when he "all alone was riding the keel of his ship."

Now it is that we first meet Odysseus in the "Odyssey." The first four books have served to whet our curiosity, and have provided as well a sequel to the "Iliad."

Calypso finds Odysseus sitting on the seashore

bewailing his fate. Without ship or men, how can he hope to reach Ithaca again? This is what Calypso said to him:

"Luckless man, sorrow here no longer I beg thee, nor pine away. Ready and willing I am even now to speed thee hence. So come, rise, and with an axe hew long beams and build a broad raft, fastening upon it cross-planks to make a raised deck, that it may carry thee over the misty deep. Therein will I stow bread and water and red wine such as will satisfy thy heart, to ward off hunger. . . ." And right well Calypso helped him. "She gave him a great axe such as was well suited to his grasp; a brazen axe it was, double-edged, and in it securely fastened a good handle of olive. She gave him too a polished adze, and presently led the way to the furthest part of the island, where grew tall trees, the alder and the poplar and the fir, which reaches unto the skies, seasoned and dry that would float buoyantly for him. So, once she had shown him where the tall trees grew, the fair goddess Calypso set off homewards, and he set to cutting him timber, and busily his work went forward. Twenty trees he felled and trimmed with the axe; then cleverly he smoothed them, straightening them by the line. Meanwhile, Calypso brought him augers, with which he bored every piece, jointing them together and securing them with pegs and morticings. Wide as the hull of a broad-beamed freight-ship, traced by some skilful carpenter, so wide was the raft Odysseus made. And, labouring, he set up deck-beams and bolted them to the close-set ribs and finished off his work with long gunwales. And in the raft he put a mast and a yard-arm fitted to it, a rudder as well to help him steer a course. From the stem to the stern he fenced it about with wattled osiers, as a bulwark against the waves, and strewed in much brush."

Then Calypso brought him cloth for sail-making. These, too, did he contrive in his skill. And braces and halyards and sheets he made fast in his raft, and then with rollers pushed it down to the fair salt sea.

It took Odysseus four days to build his raft, and on the fifth he sailed away, and Calypso sent a gentle favouring wind, and for seventeen days he sailed, and on the eighteenth day he came within sight of the land of the Phæacians (Corfu), and all would have been well had not Poseidon seen him from afar off. The sea-god knew that Zeus must have come to the assistance of Odysseus, but notwithstanding this, determines to gather the clouds, and trouble the waters, and rouse the winds. As a result, Odysseus narrowly escapes with his life, and is cast ashore more dead than alive.

Book VI.—The sixth book opens with a beautiful description of how Athene contrives that Nausicaa, the daughter of Alcinous, King of the Phæacians, should take the family washing down to a little stream, near where Odysseus is sleeping. She asks her father for a wagon, and he replies:

"Neither the mules nor aught else do I grudge thee, my dear child. Go now, and the slaves shall make ready for thee the wagon that is tall and strong of wheel and fitted with a frame above."

And so saying, he called up his men, and outside the palace they made ready the easy-running mule cart and led the mules under the yoke and harnessed them, while from her room the maiden brought out the bright raiment and stowed it in the polished car. In a basket her mother put all kinds of food, such as satisfy the heart, and set therein, too, dainties, and filled a goat-skin bottle with wine. Then Nausicaa mounted the cart, and her mother gave her smooth olive oil in a golden flask that, after they had bathed, she and her maidens might anoint themselves. So Nausicaa took the whip and the bright reins, and touching the mules, she started them. Then, with a clatter of hooves, forward they strained, never flagging, with the load of raiment and the maidens behind. She did not go alone, but her attendants bore her company.

When they got to the river they took the garments and trod them in the washing trenches, and then spread them out to dry. Then they bathed and anointed themselves with olive oil, and took

FIG. 33.—Boring out the eye of Polyphemus.

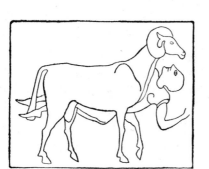

FIG. 34.—Odysseus under the Ram.

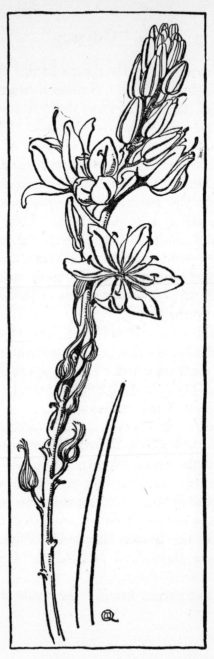

FIG. 35.—Asphodel.

their midday meal on the river's bank. After, they fell to playing ball, and Nausicaa began to sing. The ball fell into the river and they all raised a piercing cry, and then, of course, Odysseus woke up and the maidens fled, all except Nausicaa of the white arms, and to her Odysseus came as a suppliant. She provided him with a mantle and doublet, one supposes, from the washing which was now dry, and soft olive oil in a golden cruse. Then Odysseus washed and anointed himself with oil and put on the fine raiment, and then Athene ". . . caused him to seem taller and more mighty, and from his head made the locks curl down in tresses like the hyacinth flower."

She shed so much grace on him that it went hardly with Nausicaa when she saw him again, and her heart went pit-a-pat. Hearts did in old Greece. She gives Odysseus instructions how he may find his way to the palace of Alcinous.

Book VII.—In the seventh book Odysseus finds his way to the high-roofed hall of Alcinous: "Brazen were the walls which from the threshold to the inmost chamber ran this way and that, and round them a frieze of blue. Golden were the doors which enclosed the well-built house, and silver door-posts stood upon the brazen threshold. Silver was the lintel above them, and of gold the hook of the door."

There were seats around the walls with finely

woven coverings. Fifty handmaids did the spinning and weaving, and ground corn in the millstones. There were gardens of pear trees and pomegranates, and apple trees and sweet figs, and olives, and a vineyard. There were all manner of garden beds, and two fountains of water.

Odysseus stood and gazed, and passed quickly into the hall and fell at the knees of Arete, the wife of Alcinous, and implored her protection and asked to be sped on his way. He was raised up by the king and set in a chair, and Odysseus tells the king of his adventures since he left the isle of Calypso on his raft. Odysseus goes to sleep beneath the gallery. This seems to have been the place for strangers.

Book VIII.—In the eighth book the Phæacians are called to assembly, and Alcinous tells them of the stranger that has come amongst them, and orders that a black ship be drawn to the sea, and fifty-two noble youths chosen for her crew, and then after this is done, all are to come to the palace to help entertain the stranger. At the palace twelve sheep were sacrificed, and eight boars and two oxen, and here it is that we are given an indication of how the "Odyssey" itself may have come into its final shape as a tale told and retold until its form was perfect, and not written as it would be now. At the palace a henchman brings in the beloved minstrel, who is blind, and sets him on a chair close by a pillar on which hangs his lyre.

The minstrel is stirred by the tune to sing the songs of famous men, and Odysseus is moved to tears.

After the feast they go to the place of assembly, and have games of running, wrestling, and boxing. Odysseus distinguishes himself by casting a great stone. Then they "levelled a place for dancing and drew out a fair wide ring. Then the herald approached bearing Demodocus the clear-toned lyre. So he went into the midst, and round him stood boys in the first bloom of their youth, such as were skilled at the dance. And they struck the good dancing floor with their feet. And Odysseus watched the twinkling movement of their feet and marvelled in his spirit."

Then Alcinous "bade Halius and Eaodamas dance alone, for none could equal their skill. So they took into their hands the beautiful purple ball, which clever Polybus had made them, and, the one leaning back and tossing it up towards the shadowy clouds, the other would spring from the ground and catch it again before ever his feet touched the earth. And when they had tried their skill at flinging the ball straight up, then they began to dance upon the bounteous earth and pass the ball from hand to hand, and the other youths stood by in the lists and kept time, and a great clamour arose."

Everyday Life in Homeric Greece

Then the kindly Alcinous suggested that the twelve princes who ruled under him should join in giving a stranger's gift to Odysseus, so that he might go to supper with a glad heart. At supper Odysseus ". . . carved off a helping of the chine of a white-toothed boar, of which yet more was left over, rich with fat on either side." This he sent by a henchman to the minstrel Demodocus, and asked that he would tell them of the wooden horse. In this way we get fuller details than were given by Menelaos in the fourth book. The minstrel tells how that Odysseus had fashioned the horse and filled it with the bravest Greeks. To lull Trojan suspicion, other Greeks set fire to the huts of their camp, and went aboard their ships, and sailed away. The Trojans dragged the horse into Troy itself, and sat around wondering and debating what to do with it, and then the sons of the Achæans poured forth from the horse and sacked the city. It must be remembered that all this time the Phæacians do not know that they are entertaining Odysseus.

At the end of the eighth book Alcinous calls on him to tell them of his adventures, and in the ninth book he does so, and begins:

Book IX.—"I am Odysseus, Laertes's son, who am known among all men for my wiles."

Here we might ask any of our readers who are interested in telling tales to take note of the clever-

Fig. 36.—Achilles transported to the Isles of the Blest.

FIG. 37. — The Island of the Ship of Odysseus at Corfu.

ness with which the "Odyssey" is constructed. So far we have only heard of what happened to Odysseus after he left the island of Calypso, but one's curiosity has been whetted by references to the adventures which had gone before, and our interest is sustained because we know that more must follow ere he finally reaches Ithaca.

This is the tale that Odysseus told the Phæacians. When he and his men left Troy, the wind carried their ships to Ismarus in Thrace, where they sacked the city and slew many of the inhabitants, until the neighbours coming to their assistance, the Achæans were driven back to their ships.

For nine whole days they were driven by storms until they came to ". . . the country of the lotus-eaters, who eat a flowery food." This was tasted by certain of the company who were sent out to reconnoitre.

"Now such of them as ate the honey-sweet fruit of the lotus had no longer any wish to bring tidings nor to return, but there they were minded to stay among the lotus-eating men, feeding on the lotus and forgetful of the homeward way. But them weeping did I hale back to the ships, unwilling as they were, and binding them thrust them beneath the benches of the hollow ships."

Again they set sail, and this time they came to the land of the Cyclopes in Sicily. Here Odysseus and twelve of his men went prospecting, and came to the cave of a giant. They waited, expecting to be charitably entertained, but when the giant returned, and threw down a great log for the fire, Odysseus and his men fled into the back of the cavern, while the giant blocked the door with a great stone, and then made preparations for his supper. Soon he saw the Achæans and, notwithstanding the explanations of Odysseus, "he answered not at all; but, springing up, he laid hands upon my comrades, and grasping two of them at once, dashed them against the earth as they might have been puppies, so their brains ran out upon the ground and the earth was wet with them. Then he carved them limb from limb, and made ready his supper. Like a mountain-bred lion he ate, and stinted not; for the entrails he ate as well as the flesh and also the bones with their marrow." Then the giant slept. In the morning two more of the men were devoured, and the giant went out, putting the door stone in position to keep them prisoners.

Odysseus planned their escape. The Cyclops had left a great club in the cave, and we can form some idea of what a giant he was, when we hear that it was equal in size ". . . to the mast of a black ship, twenty-oared."

Odysseus cut a fathom's length off this (six feet), and fined it down, and made it even, and sharpened it to a point, and hardened it in the fire.

In the evening the giant returned, and drove his sheep into the cave, and two more men were eaten. Now, Odysseus had brought wine with him, which he had in the cave, and first one cup and then another was given to the giant until he at last became drunk. Before this Odysseus tells the giant that his name is Noman. Now was the time for action, and "they took the sharp-pointed stake of olive-wood and plunged it into his eye, while, bearing upon it from my place above, I turned it about, as when a man bores a ship's timber with a drill and below his fellows spin it with a thong which they hold at either end and the drill runs round unceasingly; so in his eye we took and whirled about the fiery-pointed stake, and blood flowed round the heated bar and the flame singed his eyelids and his brows on every side, as the eyeball consumed and its roots crackled in the fire. Just as when a smith dips some great axe or an adze hissing into cold water that it may be tempered—for thence proceeds the strength of the iron—even so did his eye hiss round the olive-wood stake. Terrible then was the bellow he raised, till the rocks rang round about; in terror we fled, and he plucked forth the stake all blood-bedabbled from his eye."

The giant in his agony calls so loudly that his neighbours come to his assistance and ask him from outside the cave what is the matter, to which he replies that "no man is killing him." And they quite properly reply that if no man is killing him, what is all the to-do about?

The giant then groped his way to the door, and lifted away the great stone and sat in the entry, so that the Achæans might not escape. However, Odysseus contrives this by lashing the sheep together in threes with withies. The middle sheep of each set of three supported one man, who suspended himself below the sheep. Odysseus himself used the ram in this way. The blinded giant felt along the backs of the sheep and did not discover them.

Now the giant Polyphemus was a son of Poseidon, the god of the seas, and he prayed to him that Odysseus and his men might never come to their home in Ithaca, or, if they did, only after much tribulation. This was the beginning of the troubles of Odysseus.

Book X.—In the tenth book they reach the island home of Æolus, which floated on the sea, and had cliffs which ran up from the seas with walls of unbroken bronze. There Odysseus was kindly entertained, and sped on his way. All might have been well because Æolus was the keeper of the winds, and he provided a good west wind which was what Odysseus needed, and bound all the others in an ox-hide wallet. The west wind carried them to within sight of Ithaca, but while Odysseus was asleep his men opened the wallet to find what treas-

Fig. 38.—Epinetron or Spinning Instrument.

Fig. 39.—Spinning.

ure it contained; then out burst all the noisy winds and carried them back to the Æolian isle. Here they were badly received, and driven away as being ". . . hated by the immortal gods."

For six days they sailed, and on the seventh came to Lamos. Here they were attacked by the people, who were giants, and of the twelve ships, only the one of Odysseus and his men escaped. Now the one ship sailed on alone, and came to the Ææan isle, where dwelt Circe of the braided tresses.

Eurylochus was sent forward with some of the men and came to the halls of Circe. "And round the palace roamed mountain-bred wolves and lions, whom Circe herself had bewitched by the evil drugs that she gave them. These did not set upon my men, but ramped round fawning upon them and wagging their long tails."

When they came to the palace the men went in, and Circe offered them wine, but Eurylochus tarried behind, and saw with horror that when his companions had "drunk it off, presently she struck them with a wand and penned them in the sties. The head and the voice they had, and the bristles and the shape of swine, but their minds remained as before. So penned, they were weeping, and Circe flung them to eat, acorns and mast and the berries of the cornel tree, such provender as wallowing swine are wont to batten on."

Hermes came to the assistance of Odysseus, and

gave him a herb of virtue to resist the charms of Circe, and being able to resist, he makes a bargain that his men should be restored to human shape, and this being done, they remained there a year "feasting on abundant flesh and on sweet wine."

Book XI.—In the eleventh book Odysseus takes leave of Circe, and sails to the limits of the world and the dwelling of Hades and dread Persephone. There he sacrifices, and the spirits of the dead come to him. One, Teiresias, warns him that his own death will come from the sea, and recommends that on his return to Ithaca, Odysseus should take with him ". . . a shapen oar, till thou shalt reach men who know not the sea, nor eat salt mixed with their food, nor know anything of purple-cheeked ships nor of shapen oars that are the wings of ships. I will tell thee a sign so plain that it cannot escape thee; whenever another traveller encountering thee shall say that it is a winnowing-fan thou art carrying on thy strong shoulder, then do thou drive thy shapen oar into the ground and make goodly sacrifice to Lord Poseidon. . . ."

Odysseus sees the spirit of his own mother, and she tells him:

". . . No, it was my longing for thee, great Odysseus, and for thy counsels and for thy loving kindness that robbed me of sweet life."

Many other phantoms of men outworn came to Odysseus across the mead of Asphodel—Agamemnon, Achilles, and Patroklos who had fought with him at Troy. Tantalus was there in torment, standing in water up to his chin, which always fell away as he stooped to drink, and tall trees which tossed their fruit away as he clutched at them. And there was Sisyphus, who continually rolled a great stone uphill.

Book XII.—In the twelfth book Odysseus has left the land of Hades, and his next adventure is the passage of the island of the Sirens, who bewitched men by their songs, and lured them to destruction. Odysseus was bound to the mast of his ship, and the ears of his men stopped with wax so that they might not hear the music.

Then came the adventure of Scylla and Charybdis. Scylla was a dreadful monster, with twelve feet and six necks with a head on each and therein three rows of teeth. Living in a cave, she swooped down and caught up out of the ship six of Odysseus's men. Charybdis was a whirlpool that sucked down the water and spouted it up again. Having passed these perils, disaster overtakes them, because the men kill the cattle of Helios, on the isle of Thrinacia. Because of this, the ship and the men are destroyed in a great storm, and only Odysseus is rescued by Calypso, to live with her on the isle of Ogygia, and this is where we first meet Odysseus in the "Odyssey."

Henceforward the tale becomes a straightforward

recital of Odysseus's return to Ithaca, but our interest is sustained because we know that there must be dramatic happenings when the wooers are discovered.

Book XIII.—In the thirteenth book Odysseus is sent back to Ithaca by Alcinous, and, going to sleep in the ship, is put on shore without being awakened, and then the kindly Phæacians sailed back. It is sad to relate that Poseidon had his revenge, because as the ship neared home "then near her drew the shaker of the earth, and he struck and changed her into a stone and rooted her fast to the ocean bed with a blow of the flat of his hand."

To-day, in Corfu, the people show you an island which, they say, is Odysseus's ship turned into stone. We give you a sketch (Fig. 37) to show you what it looks like.

When Odysseus awakened, he found his constant friend Athene by him, and she contrived that:

"I will wrinkle the fair skin on thy supple limbs, and from off thy head I will make to fall thy yellow hair, and wrap thee in a foul garment, such that one would shudder to see a man clothed therein."

It is in this guise that he goes to the house of Eumæus, the swineherd, while Athene hastes to Sparta to bring back Telemachus. This brings us back to the doings recounted in the fourth book.

Book XIV.—In the fourteenth book Odysseus arrives at the house of the swineherd, and "found

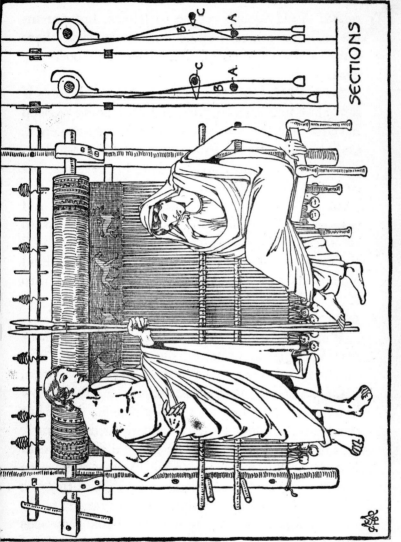

SECTIONS

Fig. 40.—Telemachus and Penelope at her loom.

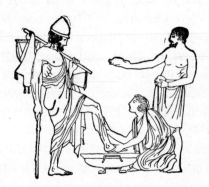

FIG. 41.

Washing the feet of Odysseus.

him sitting in the fore-hall of his house, where his courtyard was builded high, in a place overlooking a wide prospect; a great court it was, and goodly, with an open space all around. This the swineherd himself had built for his master's swine, his master who was far away, and his mistress and the old man Laertes knew nothing of it. With huge stones he had built it, and fenced it in with a hedge of white thorn. Outside, splitting oak to the dark core, he had driven in stakes the whole length of it on either side, set thick and close; and within the courtyard he made twelve sties, near by one another, as beds for the swine, and in each sty fifty were penned, fifty wallowing swine sows for breeding; but the boars slept without."

Odysseus is kindly entertained by the swineherd, and given roasted pork sprinkled with white barley-meal to eat, he hears of the misdeeds of the wooers.

Book XV.—In the fifteenth book Telemachus is brought back by Athene, and, escaping the wooers who laid in wait for him, goes to the house of the swineherd.

Book XVI.—In the sixteenth book Eumæus is sent to the town and Odysseus makes himself known to his son. To assist him in this, "Athene touched him with her golden wand. A fresh cloak and a tunic she first of all cast about his chest, and she heightened his stature and the bloom of his manhood. Warm once more grew his colour; his

cheeks plumpened, and thickly round his chin
sprang the black beard."

When the swineherd returns, Odysseus becomes
an old beggar man again.

Book XVII.—In the seventeenth book Telemachus goes to tell his mother Penelope of his
journey, and in the evening Odysseus and the
swineherd go to . . .

"The fair house of Odysseus, easily a man would
know it, though he saw it among many others.
There is building beyond building, and the courtyard of the house is closed in with a wall and battlements, and well-fenced are the folding doors."

They meet Melanthius, the goatherd, who reviles
them. Here no one knows him except his old
hound, Argos, who lay "upon the deep dung of
mules and kine, that lay heaped up before the doors,
till the slaves of Odysseus should carry it away to
dung his wide lands." Yet the hound recognised
the voice of his master, and "wagging his tail
dropped both ears, but nearer to his master he had
no longer strength to come. And Odysseus
glanced away, wiping a tear that he easily hid
from Eumæus. . . . But as for Argos, black death
descended on him in that same hour that he saw
Odysseus again, in the twentieth year of his
age."

Then Odysseus entered the house, sat down within the doorway, and watched the feast and listened

The "Odyssey"

to the minstrel; and Telemachus was there and
sent him food by the swineherd, and told him to
beg of the wooers as well. Athene urged him in
the same way to make test of them. All gave him
somewhat, except Antinous, who caught up a foot-
stool and struck him with it on the back. Penelope
hears of this, and is ashamed that a stranger should
have been treated in this way, and sends for
Odysseus.

Book XVIII.—In the eighteenth book a real
beggar, Arnæus by name, comes up to the house,
and thinking of Odysseus as a rival would have
driven him away. The wooers encourage the quarrel and promise the winner a present:

"Here are goats' bellies lying by the fire, which
we laid by at supper time and filled with fat and
blood. Now, whichever of the two wins, and
shows himself the better man, let him stand up
and take his choice of these puddings."

In the boxing match which followed, Odysseus
was easily the winner, and wins the pudding.

Then Penelope, attended by her maidens, came
down from her upper chamber to the hall, and
Athene steeped her with beauty imperishable.
"Standing by the pillar of the well-builded roof,"
she chided Telemachus for allowing the stranger to
be ill-used. Penelope's great beauty moved the
wooers to renewed efforts to win her, and "each
man sent a henchman to bring his gifts. For

107

Antinous his henchman bare a broidered robe, great and very fair, wherein were golden brooches, twelve in all, fitted with well-bent clasps. And the henchman straightway bare for Eurymachus a golden chain of curious work, strung with amber beads, shining like the sun. And his squires bare for Eurydamas a pair of ear-rings with three drops well wrought, and much grace shone from them. And out of the house of Peisander, the prince, the son of Polyctor, the squire brought a necklet, a very lovely jewel. And likewise the Achæans brought each one some other beautiful gift."

Then follows an amusing touch. Odysseus rejoiced that Penelope had tricked the wooers in this way. When Penelope retired with the gifts, the wooers turned to dancing. "Presently they set up three braziers in the hall to light them, and on these they piled firewood all around, faggots long seasoned and dry, new split with the axe. And midway by the braziers they placed torches, and the maids of brave-hearted Odysseus held up the lights in turn." Odysseus tells the maidens to go to their quarters and twist yarn, or card wool, but they only laugh, and the wooers fall to taunting Odysseus and then go home.

Book XIX.—In the nineteenth book Odysseus arranges with Telemachus to remove the arms out of the hall, and tells him how he is to explain to the wooers that this has been done in case they

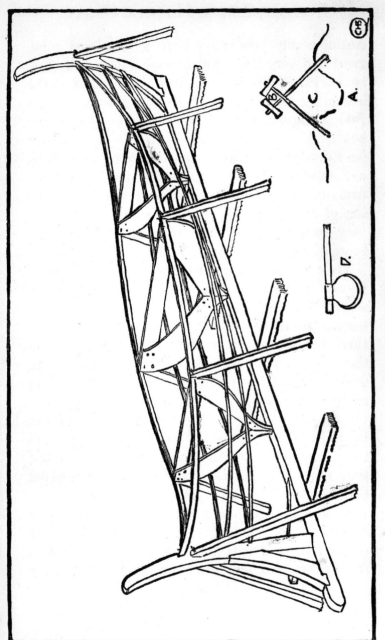

FIG. 42.—Boatbuilding.

Fig. 43.—Homeric Lock.

KEY

Fig. 44.

Odysseus shooting the wooers.

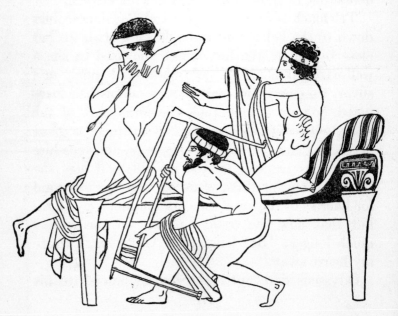

Fig. 45.—The slaying of the wooers.

quarrel between themselves and wound one another, "for iron draws a man unto it of itself."

This is the first reference to iron weapons—hitherto we have only heard of bronze. The good nurse Euryclea was called in to assist, and the arms are taken to the armoury, and Pallas Athene carried a light, and its radiance caused Telemachus to wonder.

"Truly, father, a great marvel is this which mine eyes behold; surely the walls of the house and the fair roof beams and the cross-beams of pine, and the pillars that reach aloft glow as it were with the light of a blazing fire. No doubt some god is within doors, one of those that hold the wide heaven."

Telemachus retires to rest, and Penelope comes down to the hall, "and they placed a chair for her close by before the fire, where she used to sit; a well-wrought chair it was, inlaid with ivory and silver, that once the craftsman Icmalius had fashioned, joining a foot-stool, that was part of the chair, whereover they were wont to spread a great fleece." Penelope talks to Odysseus, and tells him how she is plagued by the wooers, and how she tricked them for three years by weaving a shroud for Laertes by day, and then unravelling it by night, but that now she could not put off the wooers much longer: "But longing for Odysseus, I waste my heart away."

Odysseus dare not make himself known to his

wife, so tells her "many a false tale in the seeming of the truth," but warns her that her husband is at hand. Penelope can hardly hope that this is true, and sends for the old nurse Euryclea to wash his feet, and the nurse recognises Odysseus by a scar on his leg, left from an old hunting wound. Penelope does not notice the recognition. She tells Odysseus how she will make trial of the wooers in the morning.

"I am about to ordain for a contest those axes that he was wont to set up in a row in his halls, like oaken props in shipbuilding, twelve of them in all; he would stand far off and shoot his arrow through them every one. This contest I will now appoint the wooers: him who shall most easily string the bow in his hands, and shoot through all twelve axes, him will I follow and forsake this house, this house of my wedding; so fair it is and filled with livelihood, that methinks I shall still remember, aye, even though it be in a dream."

Penelope then goes to her upper chamber.

Book XX.—In the twentieth book Odysseus sleeps in the vestibule of the house, and in the morning the wooers come to resume their feastings, and Athene stirs them to wrath against Odysseus.

Book XXI.—In the twenty-first book Penelope descends the tall staircase of her chamber, takes the well-bent key of bronze with an ivory handle, and goes to the treasure chamber. "Then quickly she loosed the strap from the handle of the door and in she thrust the key, and with a sure aim shot back the bolts." There she finds the back-bent bow of Odysseus, with its quiver and arrows. These she takes to the wooers in the hall, and arranges a contest for them with herself as the prize, saying:

"Whoso shall most readily string the bow in his hands and shoot through every one of the twelve axes, him will I follow and with him forsake this house."

Telemachus sets up the axes. "First he dug a trench, and in it set up the axes, one long trench for them all, making it straight to the line, and round them stamping down the earth."

He then tries to string the bow, but fails, and after him Leiodes, with the same result. Antinous, another of the wooers, then commands the goatherd:

"Come now, Melanthius, light us a fire in the hall, and put a great settle by the fire and a fleece covering it, and bring forth from within a great ball of lard, that we young men may warm the bow and grease it with the fat, and so make trial of it and bring an end of the contest." But the fire and the lard do not help, and the wooers fail one by one to bend the bow. While this is going on, Odysseus draws the neatherd and the swineherd from the hall, and after testing them makes himself known to them. He arranges their return to the hall separately, and tells Eumæus, the swineherd, to contrive that the bow is handed to him and "bid the women bar the well-fitting doors of their hall. If any of them hear the sound of groaning or the din of men within our walls, let them not run forth, but stay where they are in silence at their work."

Philœtius, the neatherd, is told "to bolt and bar the outer gate of the courtyard, and quickly tie the knot."

The wooers by this time have all made trial and failed to string the bow, so Odysseus asks that he may be allowed to try, but this enrages the wooers. Telemachus sends his mother from the hall to her upper chamber, and the bow is given to Odysseus, and the swineherd warns the nurse Euryclea to bar the doors of the women's chambers, and the neatherd hastes silently and closes the gates of the court. The stage is now set for the last act, and Odysseus takes up the great bow, and "even as when a man who is skilled at playing the lyre and in song easily stretches a string about a new peg, tying the twisted sheep-gut at either end, even so did Odysseus straightway bend the great bow without effort, and taking it in his right hand he tested the bow string, which hummed sweetly at his touch, in tone like a swallow." And great grief comes upon the wooers. Odysseus then takes one

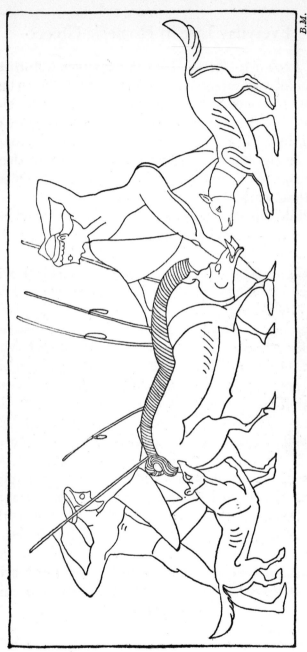

Fig. 46.—A Boar Hunt.

B.M.

Fig. 47.—Draughts.

of the arrows, and "with straight aim let fly the arrow; not one of the axes did it miss; but starting from the first axe-handle, the bronze weighted shaft passed clean through and out at the last."

Then "Telemachus, the dear son of divine Odysseus, girt about him his sharp sword and took the spear in his grasp, and stood by the chair at his father's side armed with the gleaming bronze."

Book XXII.—In the twenty-second book Odysseus strips off his rags and leaps to the great threshold with his bow and quiver full of arrows. With his first shot he kills Antinous, and the wooers searching for shields, or spears, find that these have been removed from the hall. Then Odysseus makes himself known to them, and the killing proceeds apace. The wooers draw their swords and "pick up the tables to ward off the arrows of swift death."

Amphinomus now attacks Odysseus by the door, but Telemachus casts his spear and, killing him from behind, runs to his father. . . . Odysseus then sends Telemachus for arms, and he goes "forth to the chamber where his famous weapons lay stored." There he takes four helmets and shields and eight spears. That is, a helmet and shield and two spears each for Odysseus, Telemachus, the swineherd, and the neatherd, who fight on their side.

The poem now becomes of great architectural interest, and we should like our readers to take careful note of the details which we will endeavour to explain later.

"Now, in the well-built wall there was a certain postern raised above the floor, and there, by the topmost level of the threshold of the stablished hall, was a way into a passage, shut by well-fitted folding doors. So Odysseus bade the goodly swineherd stand near by and watch this postern, for thither was there but one approach."

One of the wooers then asks if anyone can climb up to the postern, the ordinary approach being guarded, and raise a cry for assistance. Melanthius, the goatherd, who fights on the side of the wooers, thinks this is impossible, but volunteers to climb "by the clerestory of the hall to the inner chambers of Odysseus." There he finds twelve helmets, shields, and spears, and brings them back to the wooers. How he manages to get back we are not told. It was the same chamber, because Telemachus remembers that he left the door open. The door must have been visible from the hall, because Telemachus says that one of the wooers must have been quick enough to spy it. Melanthius makes another trip, and Eumæus and the neatherd are sent to catch him, which they do, and after binding, pull him up and leave him dangling from the roof beams.

Then Athene comes to the assistance of Odysseus and "darted up into the roof timbers of the murky

hall, like a swallow in its flight, and there sat down."
And the wooers cast their spears in vain. Then
the company of Odysseus "set upon the wooers, and
right and left they smote them through the hall,
and there a hideous moaning arose as their heads
were smitten, and all the floor ran with blood."

Only the minstrel Phemius and the henchman
Medon are spared, and go out and sit by the altar.
Telemachus is sent to call the old nurse, Euryclea,
and Odysseus tells her to send women to clean the
hall, and as well demands the names of the maids
who have dishonoured themselves with the wooers.
Then Odysseus tells Telemachus to slay the
maidens, and they were led forth from the stablished hall to a "narrow space between the vaulted
chamber and the stout fence of the courtyard."
A ship's cable was tied to a great pillar, and around
the vaulted room, and nooses were placed around
the necks of the women and they were hanged on
the cable, and "for a little while they writhed with
their feet, but not for long."

Then they washed and purified the house with
burning sulphur, and "the adventure was over."

Book XXIII.—In the twenty-third book the old
nurse goes up to Penelope's chamber to tell her the
good news of Odysseus's return, but Penelope
thinks the nurse is distraught, and refuses to believe her. However, she goes down from her upper
chamber and enters the hall by the threshold of

stone, and sits down over against Odysseus in the
light of the fire, and still finds it difficult to believe
that this stranger in vile raiment can be her noble
husband who left her twenty years before. Telemachus rebukes her for her doubt, and Odysseus
waits for her to speak to him. Athene comes to his
assistance, because, after he had bathed and taken
new clothes, she sheds great beauty on him and
restores his youth—so in the end Penelope knows
that verily it is her own husband who has come
back.

In the morning Odysseus rouses Telemachus, the
neatherd, and the swineherd, and goes to see his
old father, Laertes, who lives in a farm outside the
city. "He was clothed in a filthy tunic, patched
and unseemly, with cobbled leggings of ox-hide
bound about his shanks to guard against the
scratches of the thorns, and long sleeves over his
hands because of the brambles, and on his head
he wore a goatskin cap." There they find him dig-
ging about a plant, and Odysseus makes himself
known. Laertes asks for a manifest token that he
might be assured, and Odysseus shows him the scar
from the boar's tusk, and the trees in the garden
that were given to him when a child for his own.
Then Laertes knows that his son has come back,
and they all go into his house and feast.

Meanwhile news of the slaughter of the wooers
has got abroad, and their friends arm themselves

to take vengeance on Odysseus. Here we think
Homer must have been at some pains to round off
his tale in a proper way. It is quite obvious that
there could be no more killing after the slaughter
of the wooers; yet the vengeance of their friends
must be satisfied. So the poet makes Athene
speak to Father Zeus, who proposes that Odysseus
shall be king all his days, and oblivion descend on
the avengers so that they forget the slaying of their
children and brethren. This would be a char-
acteristically modern happy ending; but it would
not have suited Homer's listeners. He makes the
avengers start out against Odysseus, and they come
to the house of Laertes while the feast is in progress, and Odysseus and his son rise up and put on
their harness, and the old man is happy and says:

"What a day is this for me, ye kind gods; yea, a
happy man am I! My son and my son's son are
vying with one another in bravery."

And the grey-eyed goddess Athene takes com-
passion on Laertes; she breathes into him great
strength, and his age falls away from him. He is
young once again, and catching up a spear hurls
it at Eupeithes and kills him, and then, and not
till then, is oblivion allowed to fall on all the people,
so that they can live happily ever after.

CHAPTER IV

EVERYDAY THINGS

WE hope our outlines will be sufficient to give such of our readers as do not know the poems a general idea of the "Voyage of the Argonauts," the "Iliad," and the "Odyssey." Just as the voyage was in all probability a poetical account of the search of early Bronze Age men for gold, so the "Iliad" may have been the history of a war waged for the purpose of trade.

If our map (Fig. 6) is consulted, it will be seen what an important position Troy occupied. It commanded the entrance to the Black Sea, and it may be that Greece imported corn from there in Homeric times, as she did later in the Peloponnesian War. Agamemnon perhaps was forced to attack Troy, because the Trojans were interfering with his food supplies. If, like the Greeks, we accept Homer as a historian, we must as well remember that he was a great poet, and his telling of a trade dispute had to be glorified by the radiance of Helen and her beauty. In the same way Odysseus could

Everyday Things

not sail straight back after the war. Poems were
not written that way in olden days. Heroes went,
willy-nilly, in search of adventure, and the poet
had to give good measure and running over.

The date of the Trojan War is placed about
1200 B.C., that is, just before Greece was overrun
by the Dorians from the north. These Dorians
were fierce and warlike, and overthrew the civilisation which had been built up on the mainland of
Greece after the fall of Cnossos. It was, in fact,
a very close parallel to what happened to Roman-
ised Britain, when we were invaded by the Angles,
Saxons, and Jutes.[1] Both the Dorians and the
Saxons were unable to maintain the essential ser-
vices of a highly organised state, so both periods
were followed by Dark Ages of which we know
nothing at all.

We do not know when Homer lived or wrote,
but in all probability it was about the ninth or
tenth century B.C., when the Dark Age in Greece
was coming to an end. His part was to gather all
the legends together and form them into a glorious
whole. He sang of a Golden and Heroic Age, and
his poems, which became the Bible of the Greeks,
must have played a great part in the wonderful
renaissance of classical times.

We have so far illustrated the incidents of the
"Iliad" and "Odyssey" by drawings made from

[1] "E.L.," IV.

Greek vases. These have been drawn mostly from black figure vases which date from the sixth century B.C. This must be borne in mind. Our illustrations do not give our ideas, but show what the sixth-century Greek accepted as being right.

Now we propose to try and gather the details of everyday life together, and fit them against a background. We shall begin with those early buildings in Greece, which, in architecture, are described as of the Mycenæan period.

If we enter Greece at the head of the Argolic Gulf, we come to a very wonderful group of places. First, there is Tiryns, a fortified acropolis, then comes Argos, and at the head of the Argive Plain, Mycenæ, the home of Agamemnon. Here we shall find the celebrated Lion Gate, the shaft graves where Schliemann made his discoveries, and the so-called Tomb of Agamemnon.

The dating of this group of buildings is a problem which is interesting scholars at the moment. Fig. 48 can be used to illustrate some of the difficulties with which they are confronted. At the top of the picture is the inside of the Lion Gate, and leading from it, to the right, a path. This makes the line of the original wall to the stronghold on the hill behind.

About the middle of the fifteenth century B.C. the Mycenæans built the Lion Gate and the circular wall on the left of Fig. 48. This goes round the

Fig. 48.—The Grave Circle at Mycenæ. (Restored by De Jong.)

Fig. 49.
Gold plate, from grave at Mycenæ.

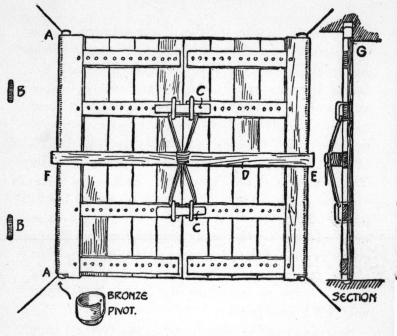

A   B   C   F   D   E   G

BRONZE PIVOT.

SECTION

FIG. 50.—Interior of Lion Gate.   (Reconstruction.)

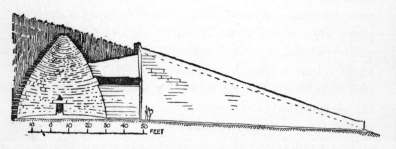

10 0 10 20 30 40 50 FEET

FIG. 52.—Section through the Tomb of Agamemnon.

grave circle, in the middle of the picture, which enclosed the shaft graves where Schliemann made his great discovery. The date coincides with the fall of Cnossos (p. 23) and the end of the Cretan supremacy. It seems as if the Mycenæans were moved to protect graves that were already there, or which they constructed hastily to take bodies brought from the tombs outside the walls, like the Tomb of Agamemnon (Fig. 53). This latter is the view taken by Sir Arthur Evans in his recent books on the "Tombs of Mycenæ." We cannot here even summarise the many arguments, but if our readers think of the Lion Gate as having been built about 1450 B.C., and the Tomb of Agamemnon some century or so before, we do not think they will be far wrong.

Seventeen bodies were found in the Grave Circle at Mycenæ—eleven men and six women; they had been buried wearing much jewellery and their faces covered with golden masks. Fig. 49 shows a gold plate from one of the graves, which has a pattern on it very like that carved on the Anglo-Saxon font at Deerhurst, Glos.[1] Schliemann thought that he had discovered the grave of Agamemnon, and he telegraphed to the German Emperor, "I have gazed on the face of Agamemnon."

The Lion Gateway is a wonderful architectural composition, expressing strength and dignity, and

[1] See Fig. 41, "E.L.," IV.

the lions are notable as being the first example of
Greek sculpture. These have never been buried,
and stand up as proudly to-day as they did when
first put up. Originally the heads were probably
of bronze, and fixed to the dowel holes, which can
be seen on the neck of the right-hand lion. A cast
of the group can be seen in the Gallery of Casts at
the British Museum. The builders seem to have
left a triangular void to keep the weight of the wall
from the lintel under, and then have filled in the
space with the lions as a decorative feature; but
they need not have been alarmed, as the lintel is
16 ft. 6 in. long and 3 ft. 6 in. high and 8 ft. deep.
The walling is called Cyclopean, because it seems
as if it could only have been built by a race of
gigantic Cyclopes like Polyphemus. It should be
noted that between the lions a small column of
Minoan character has been carved by the sculptor.

Fig. 50 is a reconstruction of the gateway inside.
The wooden doors are not there now, but the pivot
holes in which they turned are, and the bolt holes
at E and F, and two other holes into which some
form of staples closed when the doors were opened.
There are references in the "Odyssey" which explain the details. In the twenty-first book, when
Odysseus is making his preparations for the slaying
of the wooers, he sends the neatherd to bolt and
bar the outer gate and tie the knot. The doors
opened inwards into the gateway and, when shut,

could not be pulled open the other way from the outside, because the lintel at G was dropped down and formed a stop to prevent this. The neatherd would have shut the doors against this stop and prevented them from blowing open again by putting the bolts at c through the staples. The bar D, which, when the door was open, was kept pushed back in a long hole in the wall at E, was then drawn out and fitted into a short hole on the other side at F, and then the knot was tied. The doors were made with projecting pins on them at AA. These were not very long, or it would not have been possible to get the door into place. If the top one were rounded, it could be persuaded to go into the top pivot hole, and then the whole door being lifted up, the bottom pin could be dropped into the bronze pivot. One like the sketch was found at Tiryns. Doors like this used to be made in England, and were called Harrhung, and castle doors were always fastened with bars in the early Middle Ages.

The great tomb at Mycenæ, called either the Tomb of Agamemnon, or the Treasury of Atreus (his father), is really of much earlier date. The form of construction, which again was borrowed from Crete, is shown in Fig. 52. A long entrance passage was cut into the hillside, with walls at the side, and the door into the tomb at the end. We have shown this in Fig. 53, with the columns which

Everyday Life in Homeric Greece

once flanked it. Parts of these are now in the Archaic Room at the British Museum, and their intricate ornament of spirals and chevrons gives one some idea of the splendour of the tomb's entrance when first it was finished. Probably the triangular space was once filled with sculpture, as in the Lion Gate. It may give some idea of the scale of the entrance when we say that one of the lintel stones is 29 ft. 6 in. long by 16 ft. 6 in. wide by 3 ft. 4 in. high, and cannot weigh much less than 100 tons. There are pivot holes in the threshold and lintel, as at the Lion Gate, and the wooden doors were probably sheathed with bronze.

The entrance leads directly into a vault of about 48 ft. 6 in. diameter by 45 ft. 6 in. high, which, when you are inside, gives you an impression of much greater size. The dome is formed, not by arched stones whose joints radiate to the centre, but by courses laid flat and corbelled over, until at last one stone covers the whole. The internal face was then cut down to the shape it now has, and as there are many dowel holes on this face, it is thought that bronze ornaments were applied originally. The stones, too, are not wedge-shaped in plan, so behind all the vertical joints there are spaces, and these have been taken by bees for their homes or hives, and they fly continually in and out through the doorway. This is perhaps one of the things you will remember when you go to

130

Fig. 51.—The Exterior of Lion Gate at Mycenæ,
with doors added.

FIG. 53.—The Tomb of Agamemnon.

Everyday Things

Greece—the great vault of Agamemnon's tomb with its cathedral-like quality, the sunlight at the entrance fading to the gloom overhead, and the sound of the winging bees, as if somewhere an organ were humming to itself.

The only way the vault could have been constructed was by sinking a shaft from the hillside above, and then filling in after the vault was built.

Now we come to one of the most interesting places in Greece—Tiryns. This, like Mycenæ, was excavated by Schliemann assisted by Dr. W. Dörpfeld in 1884 and 1885. Their work laid bare a splendid example of the fortified acropolis. This needs explanation, because it was a new type of building, and quite different from the palace of Cnossos built in a valley without fortifications. Because of the famous Acropolis at Athens, which seems to have been built to enshrine the Parthenon, we have come to think of an acropolis as being a sacred place, whereas the word only means a city on high. This is what the Acropolis at Athens was at first, and because of Schliemann and Dörpfeld's work at Tiryns, we are able to find out what these early fortified cities were like. It is quite obvious that if some of the details of Tiryns are Minoan in character, its general plan is conceived on entirely different lines, and that a different type of people lived there. If Cnossos is Southern, then Tiryns is Northern.

Everyday Life in Homeric Greece

Again, though Ithaca on the west coast of Greece is supposed to have been the home of Odysseus, it is always Tiryns which is used to illustrate the "Odyssey." It almost seems as if Homer had a somewhat simplified Tiryns in mind when he described Ithaca in his poems. He knew the place; in the second book of the "Iliad" he refers to "Tiryns of the great walls."

Schliemann's plans are generally used to illustrate the place, but as plans are not convincing to many people, we have, at some pains, built up a series of reconstructions based on this plan and our own survey of the site. This must be borne in mind. The plan is the plan of Schliemann and the bases of the walls can be traced on the site; of these there is not any doubt. But the buildings raised on the walls are the buildings of Quennell, and of these there may be many doubts. However that may be, we hope, even with this warning, that our reconstructions may serve to give our readers a picture whose details they can test by their own observation and judgment.

Fig. 54 gives a general plan, and the various parts of the building are noted at the side of the drawing. Perhaps the bird's-eye view, Fig. 55, is better for our purpose. The ascending ramp is shown at 1, with a tower commanding the entrance at 2. This ramp is so planned, that if besiegers used it to attack the city, their right side, which was not

134

protected by their shields, would have been exposed to archers on the walls over. It must be remembered that Tiryns was a city, forming the headquarters of many hundreds of people. In the "Odyssey" the swineherd raised his swine, and Laertes farmed outside the city. In times of stress they would have retired to it for protection, and driven their cattle into the Outer Bailey at 3. Here, like a mediæval castle, there would have been workshops and sheds and chambers in the walls, which are over 20 ft. thick. There is another strong gate at 4, which turned on pivots, and was fastened with a bar as the Lion Gate, Fig. 50. This led into a long, narrow court, with a colonnade at the top on the left-hand side, and opposite it, at 6, another gateway, or propylon. If reference is made to Fig. 54, it will be seen that this had a central door with a porch on either side.

This gateway is of the greatest interest, because it is the type from which the great Greek gateways, like the propylea at Athens, were developed. Architects describe the plan of this gateway as being *Distyle in antis,* meaning two columns standing between antæ. Antæ are pilasters on the side walls. It should be noted that from the inner porch of this gate a passage at A to B, Fig. 54, led to the women's quarters.

This gateway at Tiryns led to another court with colonnades or galleries at 5 around it. These apparently were used for tethering cattle in. In the twentieth book of the "Odyssey" the neatherd brings cattle for the feast, which are tethered carefully beneath the echoing gallery. If the swineherd brought some of his swine as well, one understands the echoing. In any case they would need to be kept close at hand, because they were sacrificed just before the feast. /Our readers must not be misled by our tidy little architectural drawings: Tiryns was probably a very untidy place in its prime. Geese lived in the court and pecked their wheat out of troughs, and the old hound Argos, who was the very first to recognise Odysseus, was found by his master lying on the dung of mules and kine. The light chariots would have been driven right up into the court. When Telemachus arrived at Sparta, they loosed the horses from under the yoke and fastened them in the stalls for the horses, giving them spelt and barley, and tilted the chariot against the gateway.

It was from this outer court that access was gained to the extraordinary vaulted chambers built under in the thickness of the walls. Fig. 56 shows how these were constructed, on the same principle as the Tomb of Agamemnon at Mycenæ, by the corbelling out of horizontal courses, and not on an arched principle. We shall leave our readers to discover what purpose the chambers served. If they are feeling gloomy they can imagine them as dun-

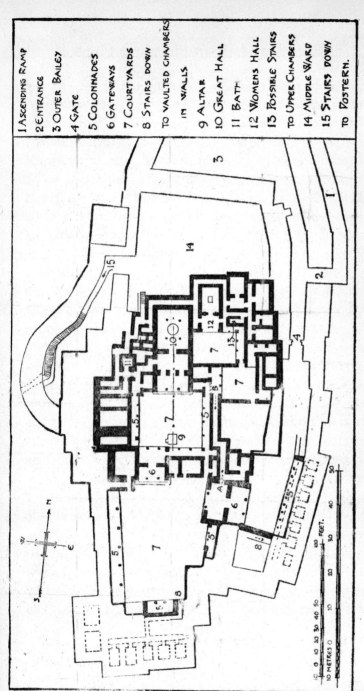

1 Ascending Ramp
2 Entrance
3 Outer Bailey
4 Gate
5 Colonnades
6 Gateways
7 Courtyards
8 Stairs down
  to Vaulted Chambers
  in Walls
9 Altar
10 Great Hall
11 Bath
12 Womens Hall
13 Possible Stairs
  to Upper Chambers
14 Middle Ward
15 Stairs down
  to Postern.

Fig. 54.—General Plan of Tiryns, based on the Survey by Schliemann and Dörpfeld.

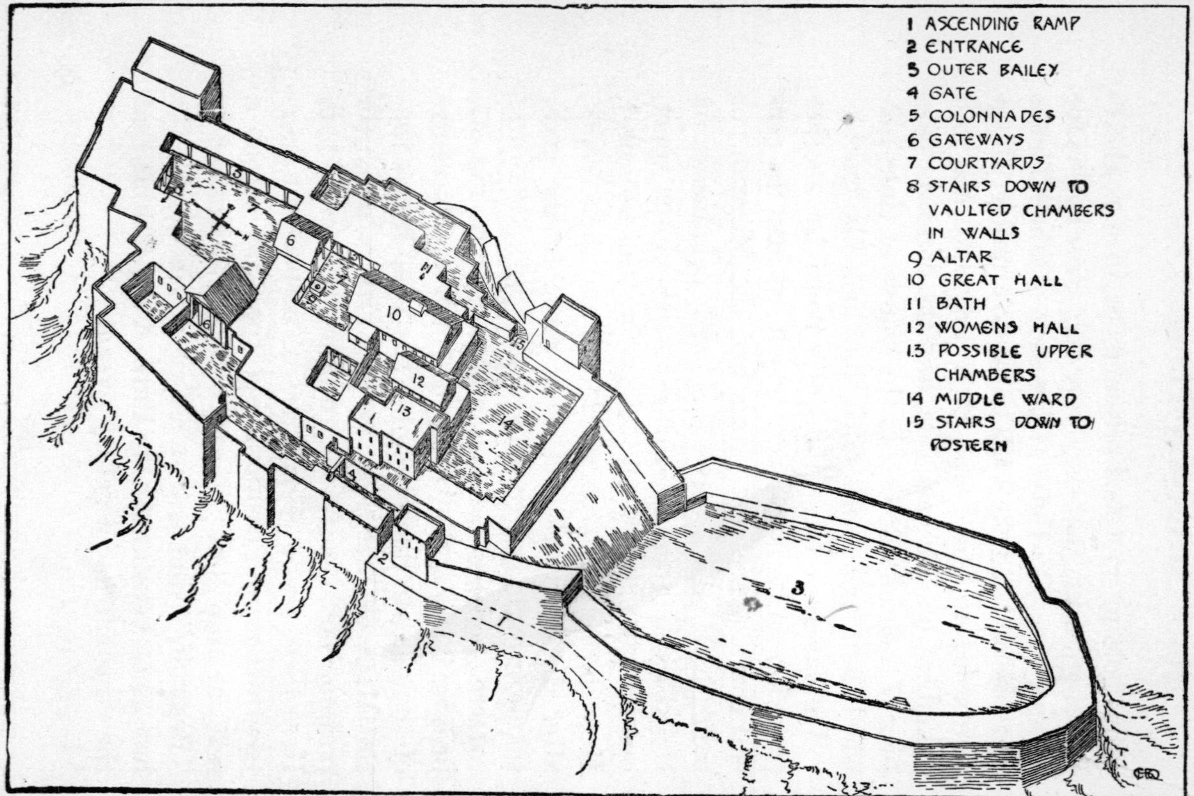

1 ASCENDING RAMP
2 ENTRANCE
3 OUTER BAILEY
4 GATE
5 COLONNADES
6 GATEWAYS
7 COURTYARDS
8 STAIRS DOWN TO
  VAULTED CHAMBERS
  IN WALLS
9 ALTAR
10 GREAT HALL
11 BATH
12 WOMENS HALL
13 POSSIBLE UPPER
  CHAMBERS
14 MIDDLE WARD
15 STAIRS DOWN TO
  POSTERN

FIG. 55.—Bird's-eye View of Tiryns from the N.E. (Reconstruction.)

geons holding wretched prisoners, or, in more cheer-
ful mood, think that they were only store houses for
oil and wine, like those at Cnossos. When Tiryns
was deserted and the walls began to crumble, sheep
scrambled up and found their way into the wall
chambers on the east side, and the constant rubbing of their oily fleeces, in the course of time, polished the rough stones until they look like marble.

We can now leave the outer court by another
propylon on its north side, which led into the central court of the city. This had the Megaron, or
men's hall, on its north side, with colonnades on
the remaining sides. On the south of the court,
on the axial line of the Megaron, was the altar.
Here the animals were sacrificed, and their bodies,
after due offerings had been made to the gods,
taken into the hall to be cooked.

Here, perhaps, we had better refer to Fig. 57,
because it shows the Megaron, which was the centre
of the city, in more detail. The plan shows that
the Megaron had three parts. First a porch, or
portico, then a vestibule, and then the actual hall.
Here there was a central fire, as at our own fourteenth-century Penshurst, but the chief sat on a
seat at the side of the hall, as described in
"Beowulf,"[1] and not on a dais at the end of the
hall as at Penshurst. We think it is probable that
the vestibule had a gallery over it.

[1] "E.L.," IV., p. 41.

The position of the bath house, on the west side of the hall, should be noted, and how it could be reached from the court, or the vestibule of the hall. Practically adjoining the men's hall, on the east side, came the women's hall, with its own court, and then on the east of this again the private chambers of the chief. There must have been a door at E, Fig. 57, with a guardroom at F, or Penelope would not have been able to make her frequent appearances in the hall at all conveniently. She could hardly have approached the hall by the line GH, though this would have been her way to the bath house, or the stairs to the garden on the north, or the postern gate.

Again, Tiryns seems to have resembled the hall described in "Beowulf." The retainers slept in the hall with their arms at hand, but Hrothgar retired to a separate bower; so in the "Odyssey" Penelope sleeps in an upper chamber which may have been reached by stairs at 13 (Fig. 54).

It is impossible to determine now the uses of all the other rooms excavated by Schliemann, but it must be remembered that to-day we think of a house as housing a mother, father, and children, with some maids to help matters. In the olden days you had your grandparents and your uncles and your aunts and the whole tribal family.

To continue our general description, Fig. 58 shows the city from the south-west side. At 14 was a middle ward, or garden, which seems to have been for the private use of the chief. Access could only be gained to it by stairs from behind the men's hall, and a passage led to them from the women's quarters. Here Penelope may have walked, and Odysseus, if he so desired, could have left the city to go on a hunting expedition by the stairs to the postern gate at 15.

Having arrived ourselves outside the city again, we can pause to look at the walls. These were celebrated even in early times. Pausanias, who lived in the time of M. Aurelius, and wrote one of the earliest guide books, complained that people in his time wrote of the Pyramids, and "Bestow not a word on the walls of Tiryns, which nevertheless are fully as deserving of admiration." The stones of these are of great size, many of them 6 to 9 ft. long by 3 ft. high and 3 ft. deep. They were roughly dressed and bedded in clay mortar. The rock on which Tiryns was built rises about 60 ft. above the plain. In the seventh book of the "Odyssey" we are told that the long high walls of the town of the Phæacians were crowned with palisades.

We will now return to the Megaron. This appears to have been framed in timber, built on the top of low masonry walls (see the sections of Fig. 57). In between the timber frames, bricks were filled in, and then the walls were plastered and decorated with wall paintings. Fragments of these have been found (see Figs. 67 and 68). The roof over the hall and portico was supported on wooden columns, of which the bases remain. The floors were cast in concrete, divided up into squares by lines, and coloured blue and red. There were three doors from the portico to the vestibule, pivot hung, but the opening from the vestibule to the hall was apparently only screened by a curtain. Of all this there seems to be little doubt, but when we come to the roof there is. Like the two mighty powers of Lilliput and Blefuscu, which Gulliver found had been at war for thirty-six moons on the question of whether an egg should be broken at its large or small end, so classical scholars are divided among themselves on the Tiryns roof. Some say it was flat, others that it was gabled. We, without being scholars, incline to the latter view.

Homer was writing a long time after the Trojan War, and Tiryns was built a long time before it. It may be that the Dorians, who invaded Greece between the time of the Trojan War and when Homer lived, first introduced the sloping roof with gabled ends, yet the much earlier Tiryns is evidently the prototype of the Greek temple with its sloping roof and pedimented ends. The "Iliad" and "Odyssey" have many references to the gabled rafters of a lofty house and high-roofed halls, that suggest that Homer had sloping roofs in mind.

FIG. 56.—Vaulted wall chambers
at Tiryns.

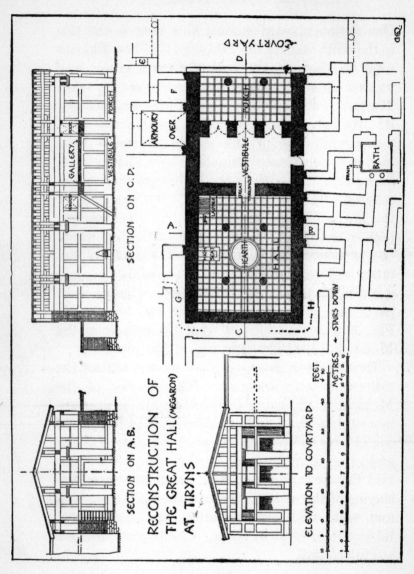

SECTION ON C.D.

SECTION ON A.B.

RECONSTRUCTION OF
THE GREAT HALL (MEGARON)
AT TIRYNS

ELEVATION TO COURTYARD

COURTYARD

PORCH

VESTIBULE

HALL

EARTH

BATH

ARMOURY

OVER

GREAT THRESHOLD

STAIRS DOWN

DRAIN

GALLERY

VESTIBULE

PORCH

WINDOW

DOOR

FEET

METRES

Fig. 47.

Everyday Things

One argument used against this view is the tale in the tenth book of the "Odyssey," of how Elpenor went to sleep on the roof of Circe's house, and waking up suddenly, fell off, and broke his neck. The flat roofers say this proves their case, but does it? We hate to have to say so, but Elpenor, alas, was drunk, and in this condition would have mounted quite readily to sleep on a sloping roof. So we think the roofs of the halls were sloping and covered with tiles or thatch. Thatch was used for the hut which the Myrmidons built for Achilles. (See as well our notes on p. 169 on the hall which the swineherd built himself.) The roofs of the other buildings at Tiryns were probably flat, and it is difficult to see how such a complication of small parts could have been roofed in any other way. Fig. 59 gives our idea of what the outside of the Megaron looked like, and Fig. 60 the interior.

Here again we must warn our readers against the tidiness of our drawings. The interior of the Megaron would have been cluttered up with many more things than we have shown. The tall pillars would have had polished spear-stands against them, and other arms hanging on the walls. We know that Odysseus removed these before he started the slaying of the wooers. Around the walls were beds and seats with skin coverlets and three-legged tables set in front of them. Chests were used for storing clothes.

Visitors slept in bedsteads placed in the vestibule, under the echoing gallery. When Telemachus went to Sparta he slept in this way ("Odyssey," IV.). From here they could easily reach the bath house in which a bath, as Fig. 63, stood. The bath water was heated in a great cauldron. Telemachus's chamber is described in the first book of the "Odyssey" as built high up in a fair court. He went to bed by the light of torches, and hung his tunic on a pin, and slept wrapped in a fleece of wool on a jointed bedstead. The old nurse Euryclea does for him, and when she leaves closes the door, and then shuts it by pulling the thong outside. In the twenty-first book, when Penelope goes to find the bow of Odysseus, she takes the key, looses the strap, and, inserting the key, shoots the bolts. Fig. 43 explains this.

Fig. 64 shows the ingenious tapered drain pipes which were used at Tiryns. They are not quite so modern as the circular-jointed and socketed pipes found at Cnossos by Sir Arthur Evans.

Passing to food and feasting, we know that the sacrifice was an essential part of the ceremony, and much the same as our saying grace. The altar was in the court, immediately opposite the portico. Here the animals were killed with appropriate ceremony, and offerings made to the gods. Portions of flesh were then brought into the hall and roasted on spits in front of the large central fire of cedar and sandalwood. Here they cooked their black puddings made of blood and fat put into the paunch of an animal. These were roasted, not boiled. The women ground barley and wheat in hand-mills to make the meal which was the marrow of men. When Telemachus sailed to Pylos, he took as food olive-oil, wine, and barley meal. In the fourth book are details of the meal he received when he arrived at Sparta.

In the twentieth book it is interesting to read how they sprinkled the hall and swept it, and wiped the tables clean with sponges, and cleaned the bowls.

Homer gives us many details of the household duties of women. It was Nausicaa who took the family washing down to the stream, and it was cleansed there by being vigorously trodden in trenches. In the twenty-second book of the "Iliad" we are told that the women of Troy did their washing in troughs of stone beside the stream. They would not have had soap, and probably used something like fuller's earth to assist in the cleansing.

Again, women had to make the clothes. The first operation was to cleanse the fleece and then dye it. The wool was then teased or pulled into fluff. Carding came after, and this was like combing it, so that the fibre of the fluff was arranged as lengthways as possible. Fig. 38 is of a curious, but

147

very beautiful, piece of pottery thought to have
been used in connection with spinning. It was
made so that it could be fitted over the knee. The
original is in the second Vase Room at the British
Museum. The little sketch, from a vase drawing,
shows it in use, with a nicely shaped basket at the
side. Then came the spinning, which was the occu-
pation of the spinsters. Fig. 39, from a black figure
vase, shows how this was done. The spindle was
a piece of polished wood, about 12 in. long and
½ in. diameter, and a little from the bottom came
the whorl, which helped to spin it. The distaff
was held in the left hand, or more usually under the
left arm, and had some of the carded wool placed
on it. A little of this was drawn out and twisted
by hand until it was long enough to fix in a nick
at the top of the spindle. This was then spun
round by the wool, and as it spun more wool was
paid out, and so twisted into yarn. This was then
wound on to the spindle, and the operation of
spinning continued. In the fourth book of the
"Odyssey" we find that Helen had a golden distaff
with violet-blue wool, and a silver basket that ran
on wheels was filled with dressed yarns. In the
sixth book Nausicaa's mother sits by the hearth
with her maids, spinning yarn of sea-purple stain.

There are many references to weaving in Homer.
The weavers stood in front of the loom and moved
to and fro before it, using a weaving rod at breast

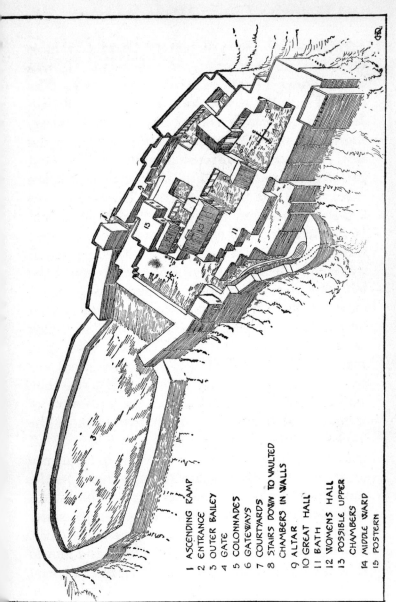

1 ASCENDING RAMP
2 ENTRANCE
3 OUTER BAILEY
4 GATE
5 COLONNADES
6 GATEWAYS
7 COURTYARDS
8 STAIRS DOWN TO VAULTED
  CHAMBERS IN WALLS
9 ALTAR
10 GREAT HALL
11 BATH
12 WOMENS HALL
13 POSSIBLE UPPER
  CHAMBERS
14 MIDDLE WARD
15 POSTERN

FIG. 58.—Bird's-eye View of Tiryns from S.W. (Reconstruction.)

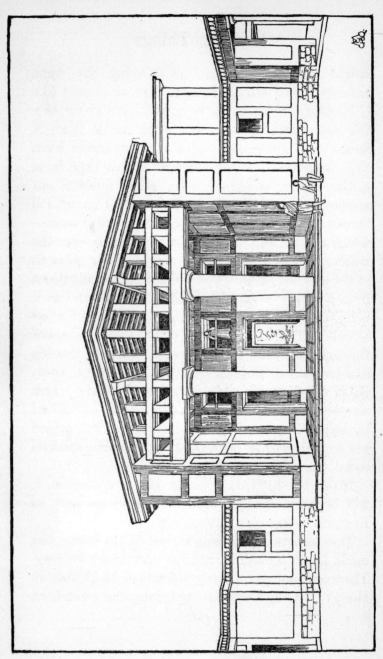

Fɪɢ. 59.—Exterior of Megaron at Tiryns. (Reconstruction.)

height and passing the spool along the warp threads. Had Homer known that we should like to reconstruct his loom, he might have given us a few more details; but from what we do hear, it seems as if Penelope used a warp-weighted loom (Fig. 40 shows a reconstruction of this type from a Greek vase drawing). We might remind our readers that weaving is like darning. The vertical threads are the warp, and the horizontal ones—which go over and under the warp threads—are the woof. How this was done is shown on the sections at the side of Fig. 40. The warp threads hang down from a roller, on to which the work is wound as it is finished. The warp threads are divided by what is called a shed-stick at A. This gives a space through which the shuttle carrying the woof threads can be passed, but these latter have to be alternated between each passing of the shuttle. This was done by the heddle-stick C, which was attached by loops to alternate warp strings, and was pulled out for one passing of the shuttle, and then allowed to fall back for the next.

If our book, "E.L.," II., p. 123, is consulted, it will be seen how we used similar looms here in England in our own Bronze Age.

The material which was woven on the looms was made up into clothes without very much cutting. There are not very many references to clothes in Homer. When Odysseus is telling the swineherd of his adventures, he mentions how, on a night expedition, the men wore mantles and tunics, and slept with their shields buckled to their shoulders, and they had leathern aprons in addition. Again, when Odysseus first meets Penelope, after his return, and before he has made himself known to her, he pretends that he has met Odysseus on his travels. Penelope, to test him, asks what Odysseus was wearing, and is told that he had a mantle which was twofold and fastened with a gold brooch, with two sheaths for the pins. The brooch had a device on it of a hound holding in its paws a dappled fawn. Under the mantle a doublet or tunic was worn.

The women's dress would have been much the same as shown on the later archaic Greek statues. The under-tunic was known as the chiton. This was simply a plain piece of woven material, about the height of the woman, and twice the span of her arms. The top third was folded over, and then the material, being doubled, was slipped over the shoulders and fastened with brooches. We shall deal with costume more fully in the next book.

If Homer says little about clothes, he makes up for this by giving very full descriptions of armour. Here it must be remembered that Homer was probably describing the armour of his own time. In the third book of the "Iliad" details are given of the armour worn by Paris for his fight with

Menelaos. Paris put on his greaves first. These were thin sheets of bronze, hammered to the shape of the leg but open at the back so that they could be slipped on. The elasticity of the metal held them in place. The cuirass, or corselet, was formed of two sheets of bronze fastened together at the sides.

Homer's descriptions agree very closely with the armour shown on the figure from Dodona. The original statuette is at Berlin, but there is a cast at the British Museum, from which our drawing, Fig. 17, was made. This shows the early form of Corinthian helmet, with a nasal guard and cheek pieces. The shield of Homer's time was made of bull's hide. The Dodona figure is carrying what is known as the Bœotian shield, the shape of which is thought to have been formed by stretching a hide on to a frame made with rounded cross-bars at top and bottom fixed to a central bar. The leather at the sides, not having the support of any frame, shrunk, and gave the shield its typical shape.

Fig. 61 illustrates some bronze arms from the British Museum of the Mycenæan period, that is the civilisation which was developed on the mainland of Greece after the fall of Crete. The sword is very beautiful. The spearheads are very like those used in England during our own Bronze Age. This can be seen by going from the Greek and Roman Life Room at the British Museum to the

Prehistoric Room and making comparisons. We read the "Iliad" and think of the life portrayed as being incredibly remote and foreign. A visit to the Museum will soon show that this is not the case. Both in the "Iliad" and "Odyssey" the arms are described as being made of bronze, and iron is referred to as if it was rare and costly. In Homer's own time it must have been in common use. It first began to be used in Greece about 1200 B.C., or 750 years before the Brythons introduced iron into Britain.

The method of fighting described in Homer is quite different from that of classical times, of which we read in the pages of Thucydides. In the fourth book of the "Iliad" (p. 39), Nestor put the charioteers in the front rank, and behind them came the infantry. The cowards were thrust into the middle. The charioteers appear to have whirled about, and the battle speedily resolved itself into a series of combats between champions. It was only by happy accident that such a method of fighting could lead to any decision; perhaps that is why the Trojan War lasted for so many years.

This had been realised by the time of Thucydides, and in the battle he describes, the opponents formed up into line and trusted to sheer weight and fighting power. The danger of this method was that the right wing of each line tended to edge away, because the shield, being carried on the left

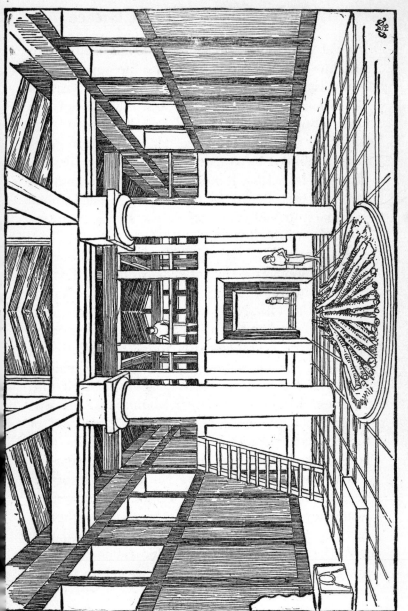

Fig. 60.—Interior of Megaron at Tiryns. (Reconstruction.)

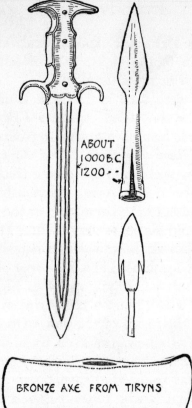

ABOUT
1000 B.C.
1200

BRONZE AXE FROM TIRYNS

ABOUT 8"

Fig. 61.—Mycenæan Arms.

SPIKE IN WALL

WICK

B.M.

Fig. 62.—Mycenæan Bronze Lamp
from Cyprus.

arm, left the right side exposed, and the tendency
was to move to the right; so each left wing ran
the danger of being outflanked.

Bowmen were used in Homeric times. In the
fourth book of the "Iliad" we hear of Pandaros and
his bow, made from ibex horns, 16 palms in length,
cunningly joined together. This does not mean
that the bow was made by joining the two horns'
ends together in bow form. Obviously a bow so
formed could not have been bent, or the ibex would
not have found his horns very useful. It is thought
that the Homeric bow was a composite type, of
Cupid's bow form, used in a wide area of Asia from
China to Turkey. It was made as Fig. 16. The
core was of wood, and on this strips of horn were
built up on the inside of the bow. On the outside
were layers of sinew protected by a sheathing of
bark or leather. When the bow was not strung, it
curved out as the dotted lines on the drawing at
the side. That is why Penelope refers to the back
bent bow of Odysseus (p. 112–13). The horn was
strong to resist compression, and the sinew stood
tension well. This is why Odysseus left his bow
at home; the damp of the sea air would have destroyed it. It explains as well the methods of the
wooers when they tried to string the bow. Antinous told the goatherd to light a fire and bring a
ball of lard, because he thought that the heat and
the grease would soften the bow. The figure in

the drawing shows how Odysseus did at last string it.

There is an interesting chapter on the Turkish bow in "Projectile Throwing Engines of the Ancients," by Sir Ralph Payne-Gallwey, Bart., from which we have gathered the following particulars: The span of the bow, when strung, was 3 ft. 2 in. The Persian, Indian, and Chinese bows of the same composite type were bigger. This composite construction of the Turkish bow meant that a pull of 118 lbs. was necessary to compress the horn inside and to stretch the sinew outside. This explains the difficulty the wooers found in stringing the bow of Odysseus. The arrow used was $25\frac{1}{2}$ in. long, and equalled the weight of two shillings and one sixpence. The silken bow-string was drawn back on the edge of an ivory thumb ring, and kept in this position by the pressure of the base of the forefinger, and released by opening the finger and thumb. The range was extended by the use of a thin horn groove, worn on the thumb of the left hand holding the bow. The arrow was laid in this so that it could be pulled back an inch or two behind the bow.

Sir Ralph Payne-Gallwey gives some interesting details of the range of the Turkish bow. A certain Mahmoud Effendi, who was Secretary to the Turkish Ambassador in 1795, shot an arrow 480 yards, and the Turkish bow that he used is preserved by thc Royal Toxophilite Society. It is reputed that famous Turkish archers of the seventeenth and eighteenth centuries shot arrows from 600 to 800 yards. Sir Ralph gives 340 yards as the longest recorded range of the English longbow, and 230 to 250 as an average of the English bowmen of mediæval days. He himself, using a Turkish bow, has shot an arrow 421 yards.

It is perhaps just as well that the Homeric Greeks seem to have preferred throwing spears at short range. Had they realised the possibilities of the bow of Pandaros, they might have conquered, not only Troy, but the whole of their world, and altered its history.

The bow of Odysseus was produced so that Penelope might make trial of the suitors, and this trial has been a constant subject for debate by Homeric scholars. Telemachus arranges the trial. First he dug a trench and then set up the twelve axes, like the oaken props used in shipbuilding, and made straight the line and stamped down the earth. The suitors cannot even string the bow, and then Odysseus takes and both strings it and shoots the arrow through the axes. This had been a favourite feat of his before he went to the war, and Penelope institutes the trial to find if any of the wooers was as good a man as her husband.

The question debated is, how the arrow passed through the head of the axes. In Butcher and

Lang's translation of the "Odyssey" an illustration is given in the Appendix of an axe used by Egyptian shipwrights, as D, Fig. 42. It is suggested that the axe is the part of the head shown by the double line, the middle portion being open. If this were so, it would have been an extraordinary axe to use, without any weight behind the blow. We think that the double line was the edge only of a solid head, and again, if any axe could be found with openings in its head big enough to shoot an arrow through, why set up the axes like the props used in shipbuilding?

Fig. 42 shows how these props must incline together. The ship of Homeric times was probably built on a slipway in the open. The keel would have been laid down first, and then the stem and stern posts fitted. The next step was to place moulds on the keel and strut these into position. Some few of the planks were fixed to the moulds, and then the ribs were fitted and the moulds could be removed. Homer must have had some such picture as this in his mind, and if this were so, the axes could have been set as A, Fig. 42, and the arrow shot between the space B or C. The axe-head shown in A, Fig. 42, is of the type shown in Fig. 61, which was found at Tiryns. It says in the "Odyssey" that Odysseus used to stand some way off when he shot through the axes, and if he did, it seems to us that it would have been a very

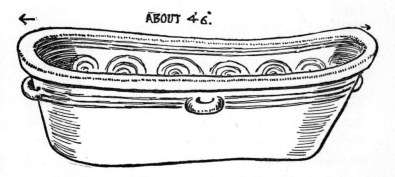

FIG. 63.—Bath from Tiryns.

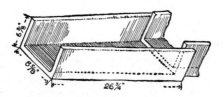

FIG. 64.—Tapered terra-cotta Drain
Pipes from Tiryns.

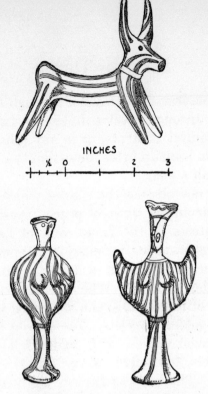

INCHES

FIG. 65.—Mycenæan Figures.

INCHES

FIG. 66.—Mycenæan Pottery.

Everyday Things

considerable feat then to shoot through B, Fig. 42.
To shoot through twelve holes, in twelve axe-
heads, arranged as struts, or in any other fashion,
would have been an utter impossibility even if one
shot for half a year.

We can now discuss the chariot which was used
both in war and in times of peace. Nestor placed
the charioteers in the front rank of battle, and
Telemachus travelled by chariot to Sparta. Perhaps the best description of it is given in the fifth
book of the "Iliad." When Hera went to the
assistance of the Greeks, she harnessed the horses
with their golden frontlets. The chariot had eight-
spoked brazen wheels, with golden felloes (rims),
bronze tyres, and silver naves (hubs), with iron
axle-trees. The body of the car was woven plait-
work to lessen the jolting, and had two rails about
it. A silver pole stood out from the car, and the
first step seems to have been to fasten the golden
yoke on top at the end of the pole and put the
breast straps over it. Then the horses were led
under the yoke.

In the twenty-fourth book of the "Iliad" details
are given of the mule chariot which carried the
ransom of Hector to Achilles. In this the body of
the chariot was detachable and had to be bound
to the frame. The yoke had a knob and was well
fitted with guiding rings. There was a yoke-band,
9 cubits long (about 13 ft.). The yoke was set up

163

on the rest at the end of the pole, and a ring slipped over the upright pin, which was part of the pole. Three turns of the yoke band bound the upright pin on the pole to the knob on the yoke, and then it was belayed round the pole; but the whole 9 cubits would not have been used in this way, and it seems to us that the remainder may have been used as a stay from the head of the pole back to the chariot. On the vase drawings there is always a line in the position shown by A on Fig. 18. In the seventeenth book, yoke cushions are mentioned to keep the yoke from chafing the shoulders of the horses. Usually there were two horses to the chariot. Telemachus had a pair on his journey to Sparta, as did the charioteers in the funeral games of Patroklos, which are described in the twenty-third book of the "Iliad." By the time of the sixth-century black figure vases, four horses are generally shown, as the diagram B, Fig. 18. Here it seems as if only the inner pair of horses were yoked, and the question arises, how were the outside pair harnessed? Modern sculptors generally get over the difficulty by using traces with collars, swingletrees, and cross-bars, as C, Fig. 18; but there is no evidence for such an arrangement on the black figure vases, and it would be too heavy and clumsy to be connected to the slight frame of the chariot.

The black figure vases, when they show four-horsed chariots from the front, give details of the reins, and what seems to be a trace marked by a cross on B, Fig. 18. This appears on the side views as coming between the first and second, and the third and fourth horses, and is then attached to the front of the chariot, as at D, Fig. 18. A short strap from the top of the breast strap of the trace-horse to the end of the yoke would have prevented it from parting company with its fellows.

Trace-horses are mentioned in the sixteenth book of the "Iliad," but, curiously enough, only single ones. Patroklos bids Automedon to yoke the horses, Xanthos and Balios, and put Pedasos in the side traces. Pedasos was killed in the battle, and fell shrieking in the dust, and the other two reared up and the yoke creaked. This seems to bear out the suggestion we have made. It should be noted that the chariot had a very wide wheel base to prevent it overturning when being driven at speed.

There are many references in the poems to games. The wooers of Penelope played draughts sitting on ox-hides. Another of their diversions was casting weights and spears. When Telemachus visited Menelaos at Sparta, he found a feast in progress in the hall, and part of the entertainment was two tumblers, who whirled to the accompaniment of a minstrel singing to the lyre.

We have already written on p. 87 of Nausicaa

playing ball, and on p. 89 of how games of running, wrestling, and boxing were arranged as part of the entertainment of Odysseus by the Phæacians. Here it was that Odysseus distinguished himself by casting a great stone.

We hear of fishermen who, sitting on jutting rocks, cast their lines into the sea, using rods with bent hooks of horn or bronze, and lead weights to carry them down.

Having by now obtained an idea of the kind of life which was lived in the cities, and by cities we mean such places as Tiryns, Mycenæ, or Athens, as it was at first, we can turn to country life. This was to remain as a healthy feature of life in Greece. A man civilised himself by living in a city and rubbing shoulders with his fellows, but he continually recreated himself by farming in the country.

In the twenty-fourth book of the "Odyssey," Odysseus goes to make himself known to his father, Laertes, at his farm, where he had built himself a house with huts for his thralls round about it. This had a great garden and a terraced vineyard. Odysseus reminds his father of the trees which were his own when he was a little child; of how he had thirteen pear trees, ten apple trees, forty figs, and fifty rows of vines.

There is an excellent description in the fourteenth book of the "Odyssey" of the house the swineherd built for himself. This was built high, in a place

FIG. 67.—Wall Decorations from Tiryns, in red, blue, and yellow.

FIG. 68.—Wall Decorations from Tiryns, in red, blue, and yellow.

with a wide prospect, and had a porch before it, and was set in a great courtyard fenced with white thorn set on a stone base. Outside was another fence, and inside the courtyard were twelve sties, with fifty grovelling swine in each.

This sounds as if the swineherd's house was like the small terra-cotta model of a house found in an eighth-century B.C. burial at Argos. As this model is of very great importance, we have attempted to reconstruct it in Fig. 1. Its date, the eighth century B.C., places it between the fourteenth-century Megaron at Tiryns and the fifth-century Parthenon at Athens, and there is a more intimate connection between the three buildings than is at first apparent. The Megaron at Tiryns was once the home of living men: the Argos hut was the home of a dead man, and the Parthenon the home of a god, not a church in which a congregation gathered. The three buildings all have the same central hall, with its portico, or porch, outside, and they belong to the same building tradition, and all had sloping roofs. This method of building, which was started by the Achæan builders at Tiryns, survived in the Greek Temple and can be traced under the architectural forms of the early Roman Basilican churches. It did not survive in the Roman house, but was introduced into England in all its original simplicity by the Saxons. From their time on we became dwellers in halls, like the men at Tiryns, until the Renaissance in the sixteenth century A.D., and that we find very interesting.

There is another description in the twenty-fourth book of the "Iliad" of the lofty hut which the Myrmidons built for Achilles. This was constructed of pine and thatched with rush cut in the meadows. It was set in a great palisaded court with a gateway. The door in the gate was closed with a bar so large that it took three men to draw it.

Hesiod is very useful in helping us to understand the references to agriculture in the "Iliad" and "Odyssey." His poems date from about 750 to 700 B.C., and his great work was "The Works and Days," addressed to his younger brother, Perses, a thoroughly bad lot, with a marked disinclination to spend any of his days working. The poems should be studied, not only for the interesting details of everyday life which they give, but as evidence of the beginnings of a kindly spirit. Beyond his own mental outfit, Hesiod can only have had the Homeric poems for his inspiration. If these were the Bible of the Greeks, they were singularly Old Testament in character. The gods were quarrelsome and treacherous. Hesiod would have understood the New Testament well, and is an example of a Christian spirit eight centuries before the birth of Christ. It was his "Theogony," together with Homer's poems, which seem to have fixed the popular idea of the gods and their life and work. First came Zeus who was the supreme god; he was the son of Cronos and Rhea, and Hera was his wife. He concerned himself with the affairs of men, and his sign is a thunderbolt. Hera was the women's goddess, and is generally drawn wearing a high decorated crown.

Poseidon, Hades, Hestia, and Demeter were the brothers and sisters of Zeus. Poseidon was the god of the sea. He married Amphitrite, and is shown standing with trident and tunny. Hades was the god of the dead, and married Persephone. Hestia was the goddess of the hearth. Demeter the corn spirit. Athene was born from the head of Zeus, and her birth was a favourite subject with the vase painters. She is shown wearing the ægis (see p. 41). She was the genius of the Arts. Apollo was the god of light, and is usually shown with a bow and lyre. Artemis was his feminine counterpart, and carries a bow and quiver. Hermes was the messenger of the gods and has the herald's staff. Dionysus, the god of the vine and vegetation. Aphrodite was the goddess of love, with Eros as her attendant. Hephaistos was the god of fire and smiths, and Ares of war. It was not necessary to have a priest to intercede with the gods. Anyone could pray to them, though in the house it was the head of the family who officiated at the sacrifice, and the hearth was the place where prayers were offered. The hearth was a sacred place, and the cities had their common hearths.

The Romans inherited their gods from the Greeks: Zeus became their Jupiter, and Hera, Juno; Poseidon, Neptune; Hades, Pluto; Hestia, Vesta; Demeter, Ceres; Athene, Minerva; Artemis, Diana; Hermes, Mercury; Dionysus, Bacchus; Persephone, Proserpina; Aphrodite, Venus; Hephaistos, Vulcan; and Ares, Mars.

Leaving this side of the question and returning to Hesiod's "Works and Days" for practical information, we find that when the sailor-farmer had laid up his boat for the winter, he started his ploughing in November. Perses was told that, if he wished to be successful, he must plough stripped, sow stripped, and reap stripped. One can almost hear him shudder. The ground was ploughed again in the spring, and tilled again in the summer. This, of course, applied to the land which was left fallow, and explains the reference in the fifth book of the "Odyssey" to the thrice-ploughed fallow field.

Hesiod describes two ploughs. In one the plough tail, or handle, was in one piece with the share beam. In the other the share beam of oak, and the plough tail of ilex, and the pole of bay, or elm, were all jointed together. Homer talks of the jointed plough. The pole had an oaken peg driven through the end of it, and the yoke was attached to this by a leather strap. Mules are recommended

as being better than oxen, and forty as being the
ideal age for a ploughman; his food, a loaf four-
square divided into eight parts. Seed was sown
by a man following the plough and covered up by
a boy with a mattock. The mattock is still used
in Italy and Greece, and is rather like a big hoe;
another type resembles a garden fork set on its
handle like a hoe. A mattock to-day in England
is like a pick-axe in form, only the points of the
pick are chisel shaped, one on the same line as the
handle and the other at right angles to it. In the
eighth book of the "Odyssey" the length of the
furrow that mules could plough in a fallow field,
without a pause, a furlong, is used as a measure-
ment. There is another reference in the twelfth
book of the "Iliad" to men using measuring rods
in a field; the rod, pole, or perch was to become a
very common unit.

The harvest was gathered at the beginning of
May, and the reaping done, not with a scythe but
a sickle.

Corn, beans, and peas were threshed by being
trodden out by oxen on a threshing floor. A windy
day was selected for winnowing, and this was done
by throwing up husks and grain with a broad
shovel. The husks were carried to one side by the
wind, while the grain fell down on to the floor.

The farm servants were to be encouraged to
build their cabins during the summer. It was only

after the harvest that the farmer, according to Hesiod, could allow himself any leisure, and then he suggests a picnic in the shade of rocks, with a light, well-baked cake, goats' milk, and the flesh of a heifer or kid. Biblian wine is recommended, but one cup of wine had three cups of water added to it.

The vines were pruned in early spring, and hay and litter for bedding gathered between the harvest and the vintage in September. The grapes were exposed to the sun for ten days, then shaded for five, then trodden in the wine press, and drawn off into vats. In the autumn timber was felled, and wooden mortars and pestles made, and axle-trees for wagons, and wooden mallets and wheels for the plough carriages. Curved pieces of ilex were sought for plough tails. The axe, the adze, and auger are the tools mentioned as given by Calypso to Odysseus for the building of his raft (p. 82). They would have been made of bronze, as were the tools used by the builders of Mycenæ and Tiryns. The axe was the great carpenter's tool right up to the sixteenth century in England. The first plane we know of was the Roman one found at our own Silchester.[1] There is another interesting tool mentioned in the "Odyssey"—the drill which Odysseus used to bore out the eye of Polyphemus. This was turned by a strap, so the

[1] "E.L.," III., p. 120.

rotary movement was on the same principle as the bow-drill used as early as the Old Stone Age,[1] from which the pole-lathe developed, which was used in the Early Iron Age[2] and which is still used on the Chiltern Hills. This may or may not be found boring by our readers, with apologies for the pun; to us it is tremendously interesting that we can walk out of our house and find a man turning a leg for a kitchen chair on the same principle as the boring of the eye out of the head of Polyphemus. Then ploughing started again in November.

It is difficult to find out how people clothed themselves in Homeric times, because there are not any illustrations. The black figure vases, to take one example, show the figures in the costume of the sixth century. Hesiod describes the winter dress of an eighth-century farmer. A frock reaching to the ground and a soft cloak over, woven with a scant warp (the longitudinal threads) and an abundant woof (the cross threads). Sandals were made of ox-hide and lined with felt. During wet weather outer cloaks were worn, made of the skins of first-born kids, stitched together with ox-sinew, and on the head a well-wrought felt hat.

Homer tells us how leather was cured. The hide of a great bull was soaked in fat, the farm people then all stood round in a circle, and taking the

[1] "E.L.," I., p. 133.
[2] "E.L.," II., p. 191.

hide up, pulled it out as much as they could. This opened up all the pores of the skin and allowed the moisture to drip out and the fat to sink in.

Hesiod thought that the farmer should not marry before he is thirty, and gives nineteen as a good age for the wife; and he would have had to purchase her. Iphidamas, killed by Agamemnon in the Trojan War, gave 100 sheep and promised 1,000 goats and sheep for his wife. The farmer is advised not to cross a river until he has prayed and washed his hands in its waters. When building a house, you must not leave it unfinished, lest the cawing crow should perch on it and croak. Then various jobs were much better done on certain days in the month. The first, fourth, and seventh days were holy days. The eleventh day was good for shearing sheep, the twelfth for reaping corn; this day, too, a woman could set up her loom. You had to avoid sowing on the thirteenth day, but you could set plants. You could thresh on the well-rounded threshing floor on the seventeenth, and this day was good as well for making furniture and ships, and so on.

You finish Hesiod with the feeling that the elder brother, if a good man, was perhaps rather a hard taskmaster. A little play might have made Perses work a little harder. A day's fishing might have done him good.

Hesiod tells us that ships were not only used for

FIG. 69.—Ploughing.

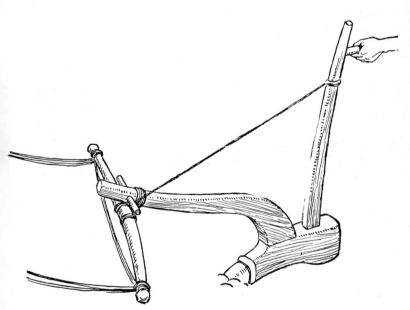

FIG. 70.—Modern Algerian Plough, resembling Homeric one.

FIG. 71.—Egyptian Ship, Fifteenth Century B.C.

war and expeditions, but for trade as well. The
harvest was finished by the beginning of May, and
then came the sailing season, when the farmer could
take his corn by sea to the market; a much better
way than by land, if the rough roads went over
mountain ranges. The farmer had to be back by
September for the vintage. Hesiod recommended
that when ploughing began in November the ships
should be drawn up on land, the keel-plug drawn
out, and then covered up with stones to keep off
the wind and rain. The rudder was taken indoors
and hung up in the smoke of the fire. The ship
was of so much importance to Greece that we must
give it some consideration.

Men have lived on the shores of the Mediterranean from the earliest times. The Grimaldi man
of the Old Stone Age, whose skeleton was found in
the Grotte des Enfants,[1] may have paddled a canoe.
Again, Cretan seal stones, dating from the third
millennium B.C., have been found, showing ships
with one mast, with fore and backstays, and well
developed stem and stern posts. The hulls on the
seals are rather crescent-shaped, and they had
oars to assist against contrary winds. In the third
book of the "Odyssey" there are references to
"curved ships," and it is thought that the Homeric
ship may have been crescent-shaped. It is more
probable, though, that Homer used "curved" as a

[1] "E.L.," I., p. 126

pleasant figure of speech, and that the ships of the Cretan seal stones were crescent-shaped because they fitted better this way into the round of the seal. For example, the seal of our own town of Dover, in 1284, took the form of rather a crescent-shaped ship[1] for this reason. In reality it must have been built on a straight keel like its forerunner, the Gokstad ship.[2]

If, however, we pass on to Egypt in the fifteenth century B.C., we do find another type of ship. Thothmes III. sent a naval expedition from Egypt to Phœnicia. These ships probably resembled those sent by Queen Hatshepset, the widow of Thothmes II., on an expedition to Somaliland. They were illustrated by reliefs on the walls of the Temple of Dèr-el-Bahri, as Fig. 71. The canoe in the front of the picture, made of reeds bound together at the ends, and pitched within and without, is the model from which the Egyptian ship was produced. The latter could not have been very strong, because, like the canoe, it is bound together with ropes, and is prevented from breaking its back by hogging by the longitudinal cable strutted off the hull of the boat. We are told that the "Argo" was girded with a well-twisted rope (p. 5), but this was probably applied in a horizontal fashion, as it was in the ships of classical Greece,

[1] "E.T." ("Everyday Things"), I.
[2] "E.L.," IV., Fig. 44.

and served to hold the ribs against an outward spread.

However that may be, our interest now is the Homeric ship, and it is probable that this resembled the one shown on the late geometric style vase in the first Vase Room at the British Museum, which dates from about 800 B.C. We have attempted a reconstruction of this in Fig. 73. The vase shows a forty-oared galley, rather larger than the one in which Telemachus went to Pylos, which had only twenty oarsmen. Another interesting detail is that on the bowl the captain is shown clasping the wrist of a wasp-waisted lady who holds a wreath. Penelope says in the eighteenth book of the "Odyssey": "Ah, well do I remember when he (Odysseus) set forth and left his own country, how he took me by the right hand at the wrist and spake. . . ."

Many details of the Homeric ship are given in the poems. The mast was made of pine, and it was raised and set in a hole in a cross plank and had two forestays and backstays; the ropes were made of twisted ox-hide, and there was one square sail. The oars, which were used when the winds were contrary, were fixed in leather loops. Sails were shortened by brailing. Thucydides says that the boats of the Trojan expeditions had no decks, and were like pirate ships. He probably meant no raised decks. There must have been something in the nature of a floor under the benches. The space under the rowing benches was used too; Odysseus put the gifts of the Phæacians there. (See p. 160 for details of shipbuilding.) The Homeric Greeks had a system of lighthouses or beacon fires. In the eighteenth book of the "Iliad" a simile is' used of a line of beacon fires to warn the dwellers around that their help is needed.

Fig. 72 is of one of the boats that bring building sand to Rapallo, to the east of Genoa, to-day. It shows how very little simple hand-made things alter through the ages. Except that it has a leg-of-mutton instead of a square sail, it might be the ship in which Telemachus set sail for news of his father. The little sketches at the top show the amusing ways the sails can be set.

Having by this time got the plan of Tiryns fixed in our minds, we can turn to the details of the great scene in the "Odyssey"—the slaying of the wooers. Here, as the subject is a matter for constant debate, it will be well to state that the following ideas are our own.

It is in the twenty-first book of the "Odyssey" that Odysseus shoots through the axes, and it closes with Telemachus standing by the high seat with his father beside him. At the beginning of the twenty-second book, Odysseus throws off his rags, and, leaping to the great threshold, shoots Antinous through the throat. To understand the

Fig. 72.—Sand Boat at Rapallo.

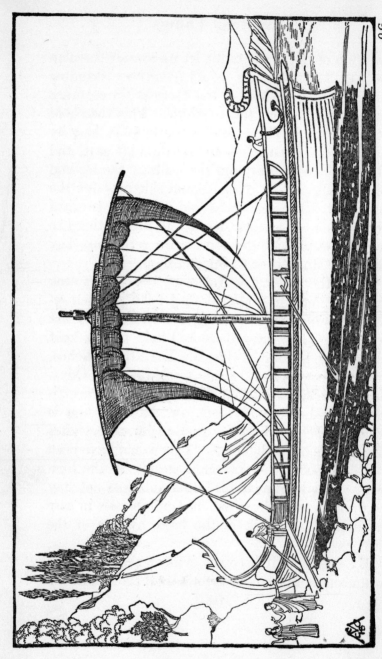

Fig. 73.—An Eighth-Century B.C. War Galley.

(*Reconstructed from a Drawing on a Vase in the First Vase Room at the British Museum.*)

position of the combatants, let us consult the plan
on Fig. 57. Odysseus would have been standing
on the great threshold of the doorway, or entrance
into the hall, from the vestibule. This threshold
still remains at Tiryns, and is nearly 10 ft. long by
4 ft. wide. Telemachus was by the high seat, and
the suitors seated around the walls at the far end
of the hall, and on the left-hand side opposite the
high seat. The swineherd had been sent to warn
the women to bar their doors, and the neatherd to
fasten the gate of the court. On returning they
probably stand near to Odysseus.

After the slaying of Antinous, the wooers seek
for arms, only to find that they have all been removed, and they have only the swords they are
wearing. They draw these and hold up the light
three-legged tables as shields. Then Eurymachus,
one of the wooers, attempts to charge in at Odysseus with his sword, but is shot by him. Amphinomus rushes at Odysseus, and close to him is
killed by Telemachus who, casting his spear, smites
him between the shoulders. This would have been
possible, because Telemachus stands by the high
seat. Now he runs to his father and does not stay
to pull his spear from out of Amphinomus in case
he himself is struck in the back by one of the
suitors.

By this time it becomes evident that Odysseus
will need more than his arrows if all the suitors are

to be killed, so Telemachus tells his father that he will go and get arms for themselves and the swineherd and neatherd. The question is, where was the armoury? On p. 146 we discussed the possibility of a gallery over the vestibule. Our suggestion now is that the armoury led off this gallery, and was built over one of the buildings in the outer court of the women's quarters. The "Odyssey" states that there was a certain postern above the floor, and, by the top of the great threshold, a doorway into an open passage, and there was but one approach to this. We suggest that this approach was by a ladder, as shown in Fig. 57, leading up to the gallery over the vestibule. The postern might have been the window opening at the top of the ladder or the doorway off the gallery behind.

In any case, the postern was where the wooers could see it. The ingenious and thoroughly detestable goatherd, who seems to have been an early cat-burglar, climbs up one of the columns in the hall and creeps along the roof to the armoury and secures arms, returning with them by the same way to the wooers. Odysseus is discouraged. He thinks that some of the maids are in league with the wooers, but Telemachus takes the blame to himself, and says that he is afraid he left the door of the armoury open, and that one of the wooers spied it.

Everyday Things

The goatherd tries another visit, but is trapped by the swineherd and neatherd, who apparently run up the ladder, catch him, and leave him trussed up and suspended from a beam for judgment when they have time. Of what happened after, and the fate of the naughty maids, our readers have already heard from our translations. And now, having come to the end, may we hope that Athene will bring to our readers oblivion to our faults in telling the tale in which she played so great a part, so that we may retire into a decent obscurity and lay our plans for a renewed onslaught on the patience of our readers.

INDEX, EXPLANATION OF WORDS USED, AND A GUIDE TO THE PRONUNCIATION OF GREEK NAMES

"E.L.," I., given as footnotes to pages 175, 179, refers to "Everyday Life in the Old Stone Age" by the same authors.

"E.L.," II., given in text or as footnotes to pages 18, 25, 36, 54, 64, 151, and 175, refers to "Everyday Life in the New Stone, Bronze, and Early Iron Ages."

"E.L.," III., given as footnote to page 174, refers to "Everyday Life in Roman Britain."

"E.L.," IV., given in text or as footnotes to pages 24, 31, 76, 123, 127, 139, and 180, refers to "Anglo-Saxon, Viking, and Norman Times."

"E.T.," I., given as footnote to page 180, refers to "Everyday Things in England," Part I.

Vowels are as in English except that the final ES is pronounced, as in Euripides which rhymes with "insipid ease." Long vowels are marked and pronounced as Fāte, Mē, Pīne, and Nōte. Short vowels are marked and pronounced as Făt, Mĕt, Pĭn, and Nŏt. Œ and Æ = "ee" in free. When marked thus, "oë," as two syllables. EU as in Feud. C as in Cane. Ch as k.

Accent the last syllable but one if it is long as Agamem'non.

Accent the one before if the last syllable but one is short, Thucyd'ides.

Note.—The figures in italics refer to those pages on which illustrations may be found.

189

Index

Index

Index

Hermēs, messenger of the gods, 58, *73*, 99
Herŏdotus, 3
Hēsĭŏd, Greek poet, 170, 172
Hestia, goddess of the hearth, 171
Hides, 48, 175
Holy days, 176
Homer, *3*, 4, 32, 122, 134
Honey, 63
Horses, 76, 164–5
House of Odysseus, 106
House of the swineherd, *Frontispiece*, 102, 105, 166–7
Hrothgar, 140
Huts, 166, 170, 173, 176
Hylăs, an Argonaut, 8

I

Ichor, the blood of gods, 40
Idmŏn, an Argonaut, 11
"Iliad," 29, 32, 45, 122
Ilios (Troy), 29; *see also* Troy
Iron, 48, 64, 111, 154
Island of Odysseus's ship, *92*, 102
Ismarus, 93
Ithaca, 32, 71, 81, 96, 102, 134

J

Jāson, leader of the Argonauts, 4, 5, 6, 13 ff.
Jumping, *68*

K

Key, 112

L

Lāertēs, father of Odysseus, 72, 120
Lamos, land of giants, 99
Lamp, *156*
Lăpithæ, mythical people who fought the Centaurs, 5
Lard, 113
Leather-curing, 175–6
Lemnos, island in Ægæan Sea, 47
Lētō, mother of Apollo and Artemis, 58

Lock, *110*, 146
Loom, *103*, 148
Lotus-eaters, 93

M

Măchăŏn, son of Asklepios, 39
Maids, 88, 119
Map of Greece, *15*
Mariandyni, 11
Marriage, 176
Mattock, 173
Mēdēa, daughter of Æetes, 14, 17, 18
Mĕdūsa, Gorgon killed by Perseus, 42, *50*
Megaron (Hall), 139 ff., *144*, 169
Mĕlanthius, the goatherd, 106, 113, 118
Melos, 70
Mĕnēlāos, brother of Agamemnon, 31, 32, 72, 76, 77, 78
Mentor, friend of Odysseus, 75
Millstones, 88
Miners, 12, 18
Minoans, 20
Mīnŏs, King of Crete, 23
Minotaur, *16*, 20
Minstrel, 88, 89, 107, 165
Mooring-stones, 52
Mules, 47, 172
Murray, Prof. Gilbert, 70
Mycenæ, Agamemnon's home, 5, 25, 76, 124 ff., *125, 131*

N

Nausĭcăa, daughter of Alcinous, 83
Nave (hub of wheel), 41
Neriton, 32
Nestor, King of Pylos, 39, 51, 72, 75, 76
Nestor's cup, *28*, 51
Normans, 24
Norsemen, 19, 24

O

Odysseus, hero of the "Odyssey," 30, 51, 57, 71 ff., *85, 104*, 182 ff.

192

Fig. 1.—The House of the Swineherd.

Index

Index

Swineherd's home, 102, 166–9
Swords, 34, 57, 153

T

Tables, *61*, 117, 185
Tantălus, 101
Tĕlĕmăchus, Odysseus's son, 72, 75, 76, 78, 81, 102, 105, 106 ff., 182 ff.
"Theogony" (Hesiod), 170
Thēseus, 20, 23
Thētis, mother of Achilles, 29, 48, 53, 54, 57
Threshing, 173
Thucydides, 154, 181
Timber framing, 141
Tiryns, 25, 32, 124 ff., *137, 138, 143, 144, 149, 150, 155, 156, 161, 167, 168*
"Tom Brown's Schooldays," 66
Tomb of Agamemnon, *126*, 127, *132*
Torches, 146
Trace horses, 165
Treasure chamber, 112
Trial of the axes, 112–14, 117, 159
Tripods, 48, 65
Trojan horse, 77, 90
Trojan War, 29 ff., 123, 142
"Trojan Women," 69, 70
Trojans, 30, 32 ff.
Troy, 25, 29, 32, 59, 76, 122
Tumblers, 165
Tychios, worker in hide, 46

U

Urn, 64, 66

V

Vaphio cups, 24, *28*
Vault, 130, *143*
Vestibule, 112
Vintage, 57, 174, 179

W

Wagon, 84
Walls, Cyclopian, 128, 141
Warriors, *38, 67*
Washing, 84, 147
Weaving, 72, 148
Winds, 96
Wine, 47, 51, 75, 174
Winnowing, 173
Wooers, 72, 105 ff., *110*, 182 ff.
"Works and Days" (Hesiod), 170, 172
Wrestling, 65, *67*

X

Xanthos, a river god, 58
Xĕnophon, 3

Y

Yoke, 41, 163

Z

Zeus, father of the gods, 30, 171

194

146